Nature in Art

Artwork of Jindrich Degen

Arranged by Eva and Alex Peck

Artwork: Jindrich Degen
Photography: Jindrich Degen, Alex Peck
Photo editing: Jindrich Degen, Eva Peck, Alex Peck
Text: Jindrich Degen, Eva Peck, Alex Peck
Design: Eva Peck, assisted by Alex Peck and Jindrich Degen
Front cover design: Eva Peck

National Library of Australia Cataloguing-in-Publication entry
Author: Degen, Jindrich (Henry), 1923-   artist.
Title: Nature in art: artwork of Jindrich Degen /

            Jindrich Degen, artist
            Eva and Alex Peck, compilers

ISBN: 9780992454906 (paperback)

Subjects: Nature in art.
           Still-life painting.
           Landscapes in art.

Other Authors/Contributors:
           Peck, Eva.
           Peck, Alexander.

Dewey Number: 759.994

This book can be purchased online through http://www.henrydegen.com or http://www.pathway-publishing.org. Also available through Amazon, Ingram, and other outlets worldwide.

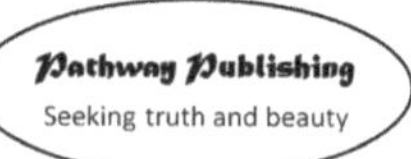

I dedicate this book to Eva and Alex
in appreciation for their work on it.

Other Books Featuring Jindrich Degen's Work

Artistic Inspirations – Paintings of Jindrich Degen, arranged by Eva and Alexander Peck (2011)

Colour and Contrast – Artwork of Jindrich Degen, arranged by Eva and Alexander Peck (2013)

Faces and Forms Across Time – Artwork of Jindrich Degen, arranged by Eva and Alexander Peck (2013)

Variations – Art Exhibition of Jindrich Degen, arranged by Eva and Alex Peck (2013)

Floral and Nature Art – Photography of Jindrich Degen, arranged by Eva and Alexander Peck (2011)

Nature's Beauty – Photography of Jindrich Degen, arranged by Eva and Alex Peck (2013)

Volné verše, Jindrich Degen (poetry in Czech) (2012)

Verše pro dnešní dobu, Jindrich Degen (poetry in Czech) (2011)

The above books can be viewed and purchased online:
www.henrydegen.com
www.pathway-publishing.org
Many are available through
Amazon, Ingram, and other worldwide outlets.

What Others Have Said About Jindrich's Art

Thank you for your paintings in which I see light and hope. I like the harmony of colours and shapes which give the impression of movement. Your artwork reflects optimism.
Ali D. (United Kingdom)

The colours in Jindrich's art are very positive, reflecting optimism, as well as purity and wholesomeness. His versatility is amazing – the way his artwork ranges from impressionism and abstract to portraits and still lifes.
Col B. (Australia)

I like colours, freedom, and the resulting joy. This is exactly what I feel when I look at Jindrich's pictures. I can imagine having some of them in my home.
Radka S. (Czech Republic)

I looked through Jindrich's art works and found them fascinating. I especially like the painting "In the Forest". There I feel that I understand the forest – being able to perceive how it lives, grows, and receives nourishment from the roots.
Drahomira O. (Czech Republic)

Many thanks for the gifts that you have brought to us all through your long life of music and art. We are all the richer for your presence! I was interested to see so many mandala-like pieces – conveying a sense of completion - though I think my favourite work is "In the Forest". Once again, thanks for the inspiration!
Erica M. (Australia)

ACKNOWLEDGEMENT

I would like to thank my daughter, Eva, who with the help of her husband, Alex, was the leading spirit behind this book. She did a great job in creating the concept for the book, as well as preparing the pictures for print. Many thanks to Eva and Alex. Their work in publishing other aspects of my artistic work, as well as their own edifying publications, is also greatly appreciated.

CONTENTS OVERVIEW

CONTENTS

Bouquet
Yellow Gift
Mother's Day
Still Life Table
Lilies Watching
On the Window
Gerberas
Fruit
On the Table
Still Life
Flowers in a Vase
Cactacae

Tree by the Water
Hilliards Creek
At the Sea
Rocks at the Seaside
Changing Weather
Bushy Hill
At Bunya Mountains
Memory of New Zealand
Sun Reclining
Rising Sun
Sun in the Green
A Little Farm

Contents

Contents

*Painting from nature is not copying from
the object; it is realizing one's own sensations.
(Paul Cézanne)*

*Nature is the art of God.
(Benjamin Disraeli)*

*Being inexhaustible, life and nature are
a constant stimulus for a creative mind.
(Hans Hofmann)*

INTRODUCTION

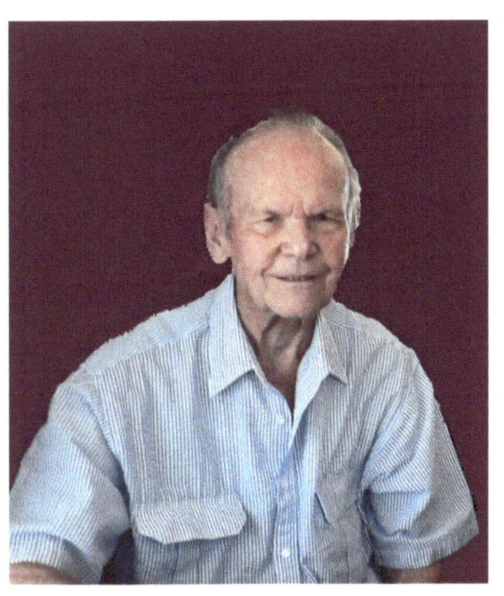

Born in 1923 in Prague, Czecho-slovakia, Jindrich (Henry) Degen has enjoyed artwork since his childhood and adolescent years. However, after completing secondary education, he chose to pursue his other great interest, music, following in the footsteps of his father, Jindrich Degen (1885-1972), who was the cor anglais player in the Czech Philharmonic Orchestra.

From 1943 until 1979, Jindrich (Henry) Degen performed as principal oboist in various symphony and opera orchestras in Prague (now Czech Republic), Gothenburg (Sweden), and Melbourne (Victoria, Australia). He also published educational music for the oboe in Prague, England and Germany.

After his retirement in 1979, Jindrich moved from Victoria to Queensland where he could begin to fully devote himself to art. There he took a four-year art course at the Sunshine Coast Institute of TAFE (Technical and Further Education). Later in the Redlands, as a member of the Yurara Art Society, he attended workshops conducted by prominent artists, including Irene Amos, Jan Jefferies, Jack Oudyn, and Michael John Taylor.

Jindrich's subject repertoire for his art is amazingly diverse, directed by his personal mood or idea at the time. He enjoys painting realistic subjects, such as portraits, townscapes, still lifes, and nature themes. Yet he also enjoys colourful semi-abstract or abstract art, where he seeks to express his subconscious feelings in images using various media (such as oil, acrylic, pastel, and watercolour). Many of these can be seen on his website www.henrydegen.com, as well as in earlier publications entitled *Artistic Inspirations – Paintings of Jindrich Degen* (2011); *Colour and Contrast – Artwork of Jindrich Degen* (2013); and *Faces and Forms Across Time – Artwork of Jindrich Degen* (2013).

Now a respected local artist, Jindrich continues to take part in various art activities and exhibitions, especially those of the Yurara Art Society. During March-April 2004, he had a solo exhibition, entitled *Images and Inventions*, in the Redland Art Gallery. In July-August 2010, in an exhibition entitled *Mandala Inspiration*, he displayed a selection of his mandala paintings at the same gallery. In November 2013, he had a solo exhibition entitled *Variations* at the Yurara Art Society Gallery in Thornlands.

This new book of 128 of Jindrich's works features a selection of paintings relating to themes of nature. It represents his artistic endeavours over more than three decades. The collection contains both realistic and abstract art. The themes include home; land and sea; trees, leaves and flowers; as well as living creatures. The last section, entitled "Fantasy", is largely the result of Jindrich's imagination.

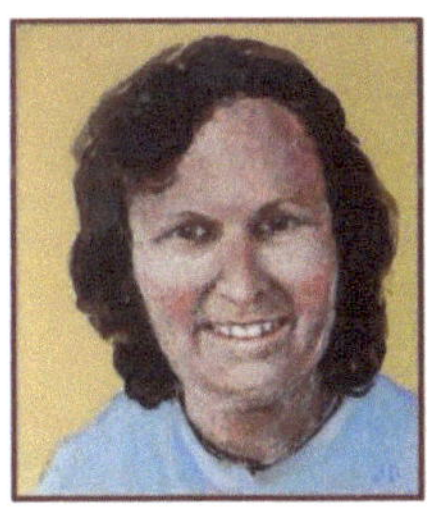

Jindrich's daughter, Eva, arranged this collection of artwork with some assistance from her husband, Alex. Jindrich actively participated in all the steps of creating this book, from selecting the featured works, digitally photographing his art pieces, guiding the computer editing process,

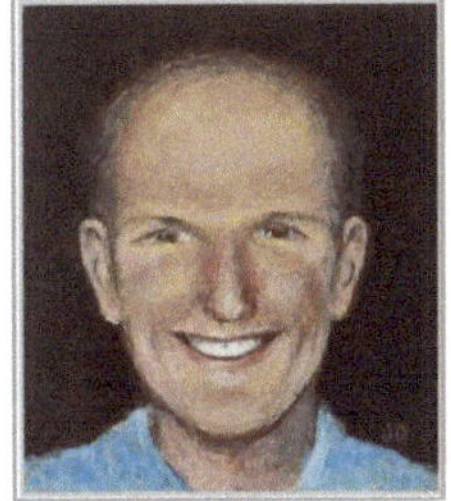

writing and editing text, selecting the quotations used on the divider pages, helping to finalize the thematic categories for the images, and advising on the final layout, including the cover design. He painted the portraits of his daughter and son-in-law featured on this page.

Jindrich's heartfelt desire is that the realistic and symbolic nature images in this latest collection will leave visitors to this "gallery in print" uplifted and inspired.

*One of the projects of art is to reconcile us
with the world, not by protest, irony,
or political metaphors, but by the ecstatic
contemplation of the pleasure in nature.*
(Robert Hughes)

*Nature is a mere pretext for
a decorative composition, plus sentiment.
It suggests emotion, and I translate
that emotion into art.*
(George Braque)

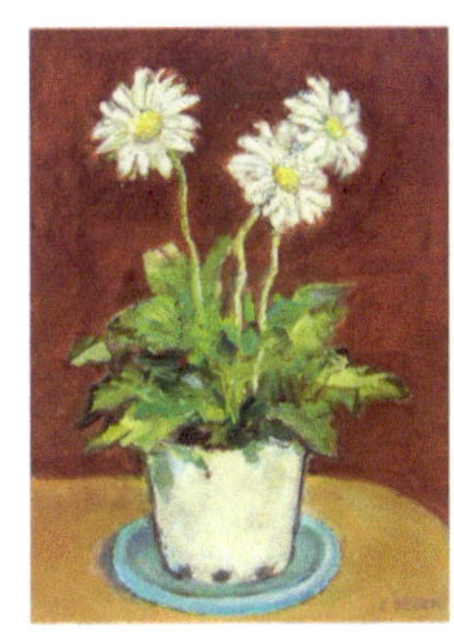

At Home

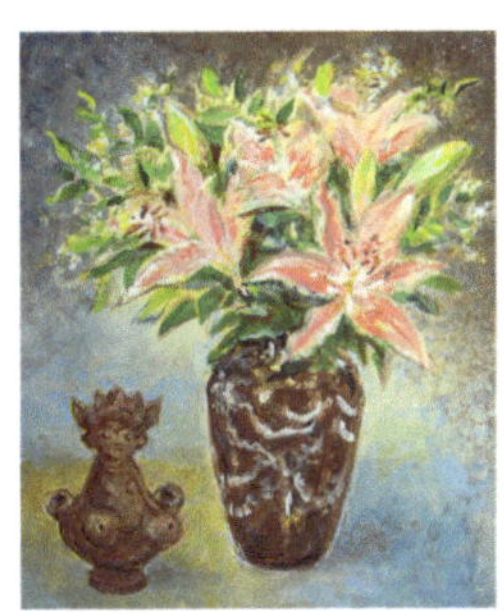

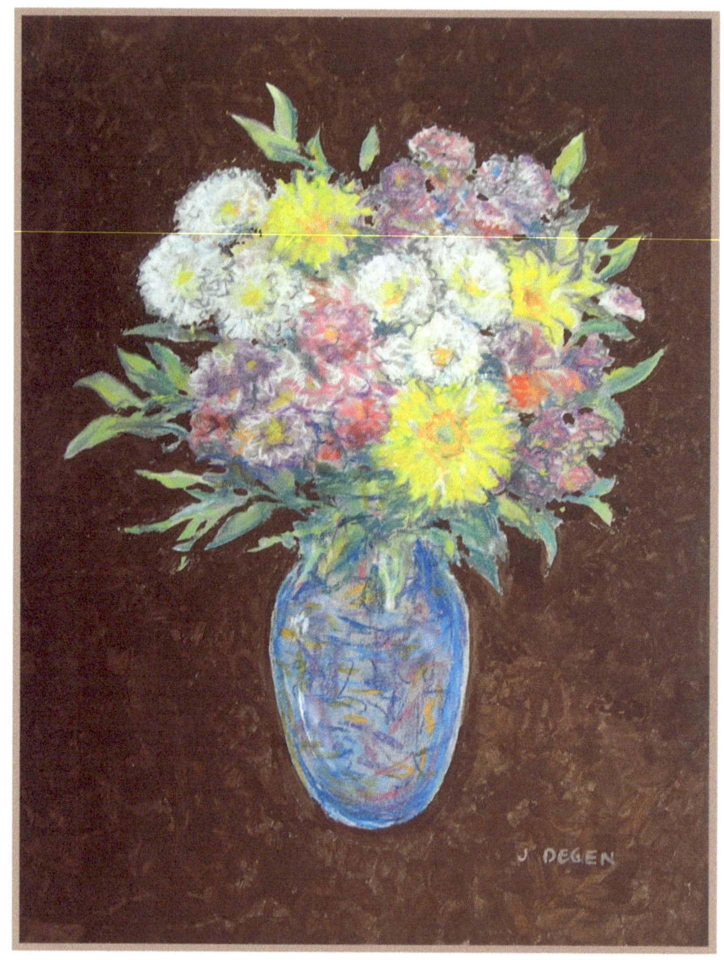

Bouquet

Mixed media on paper, 55 x 40 cm, 2012

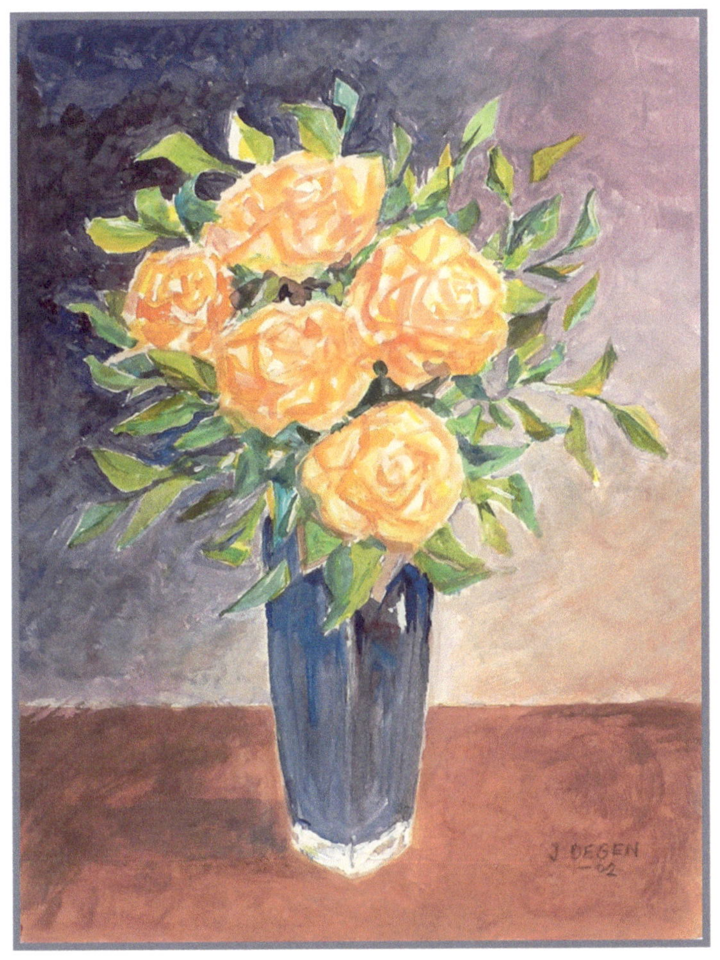

Yellow Gift

Acrylic on paper, 36 x 26 cm, 2002

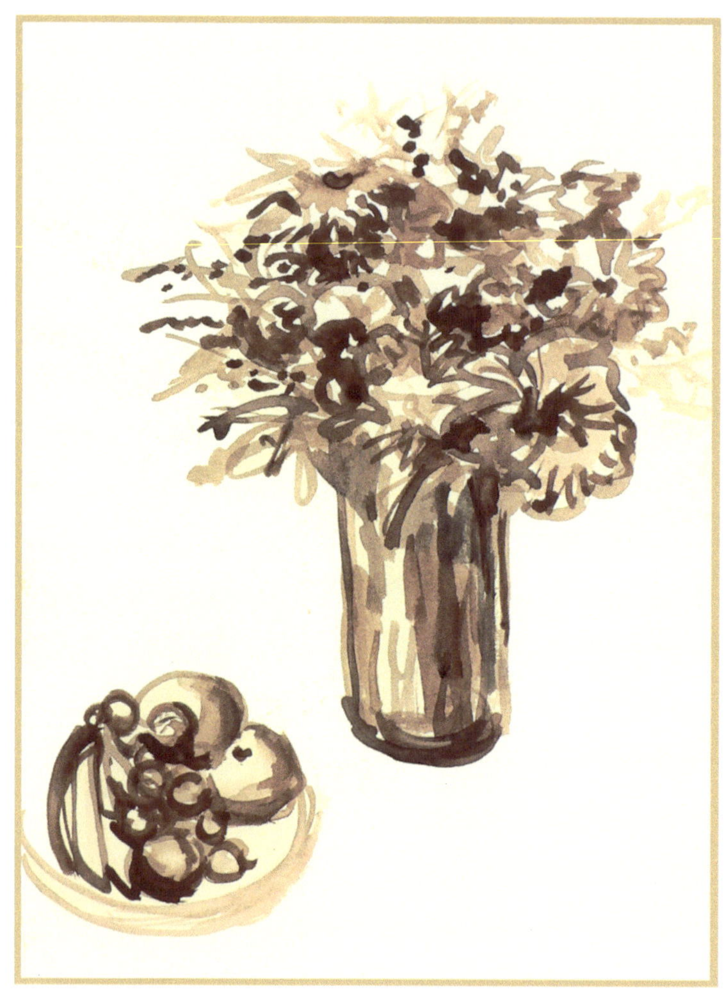

Mother's Day

Watercolour on paper, 33 x 25 cm, 2004

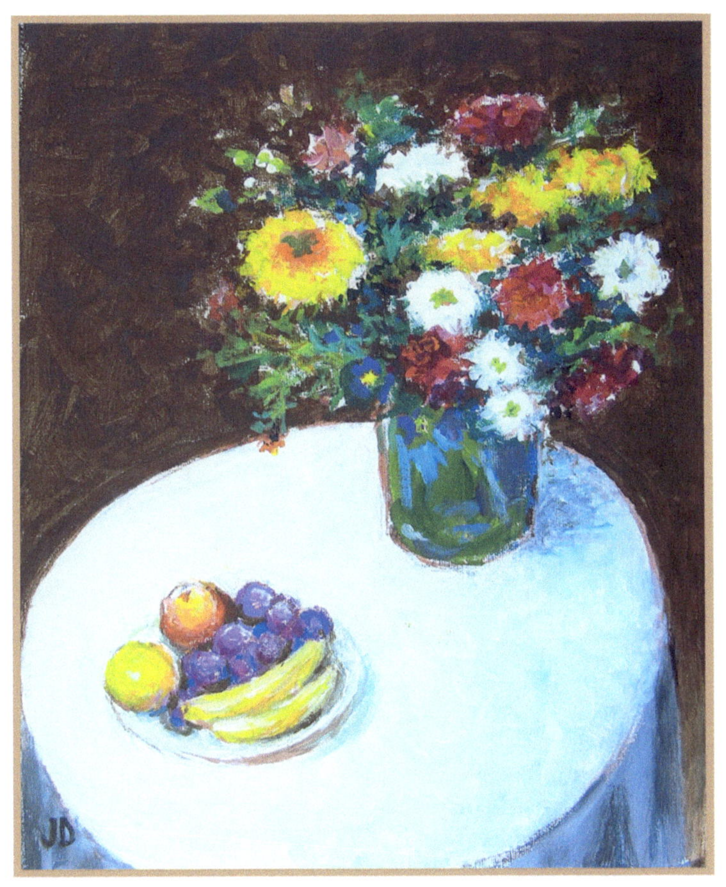

Still Life Table

Acrylic on canvas board, 36 x 29 cm, 2012

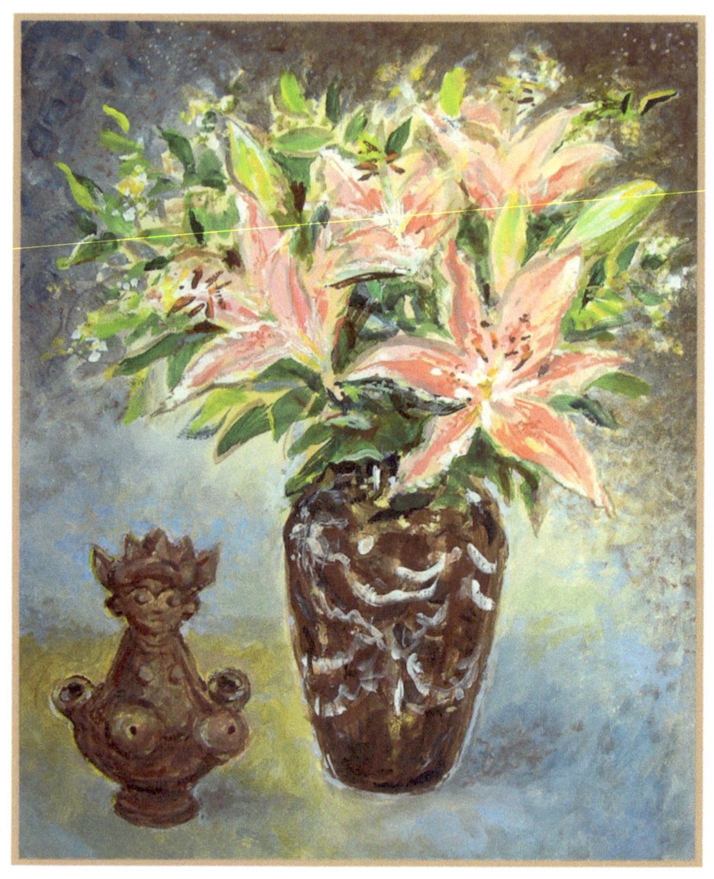

Lilies Watching

Acrylic on paper, 42 x 34 cm, 2002

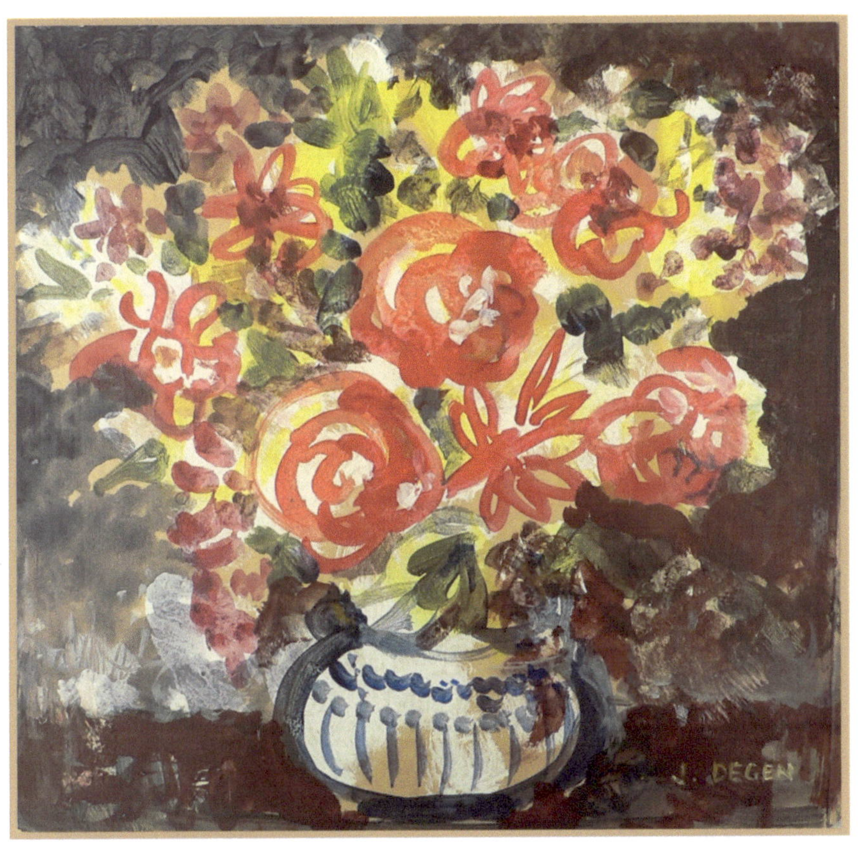

On the Window

Oil on paper, 28 x 28 cm, 2005

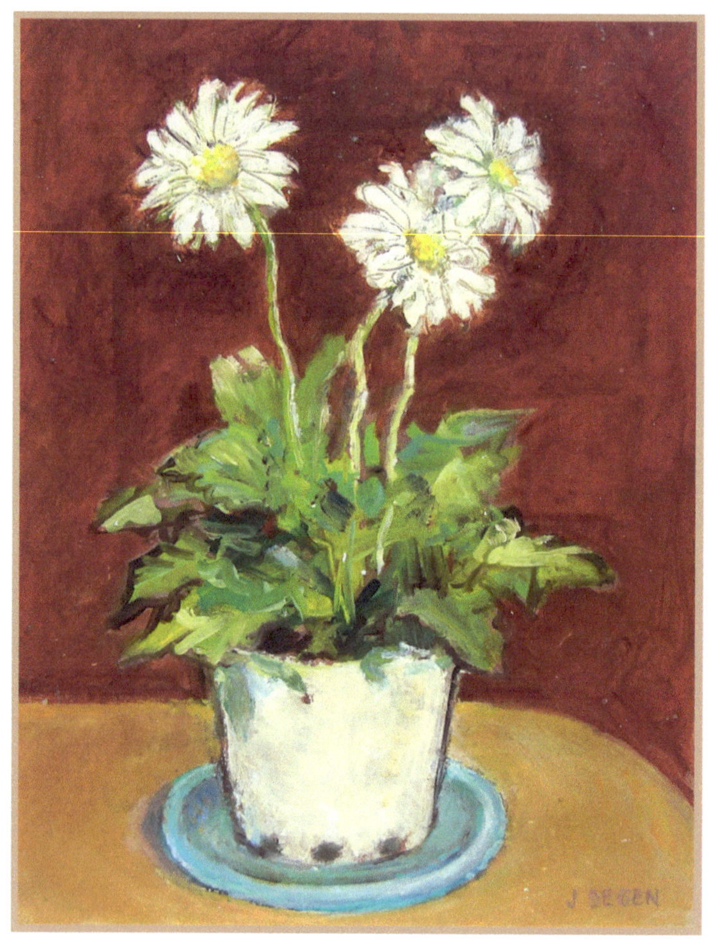

Gerberas

Oil on board, 36 x 28 cm, 2002

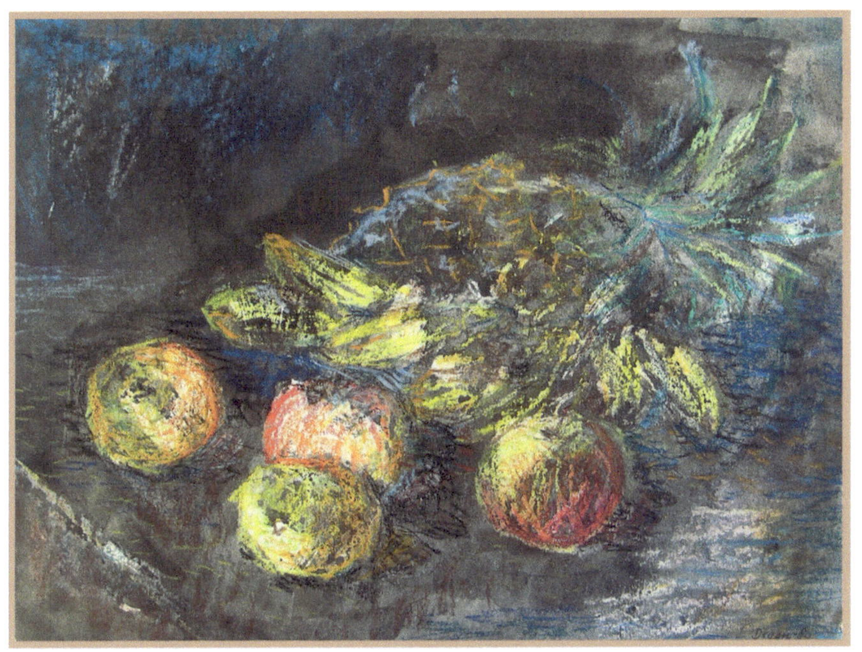

Fruit

Mixed media on paper, 27 x 35 cm, 1980

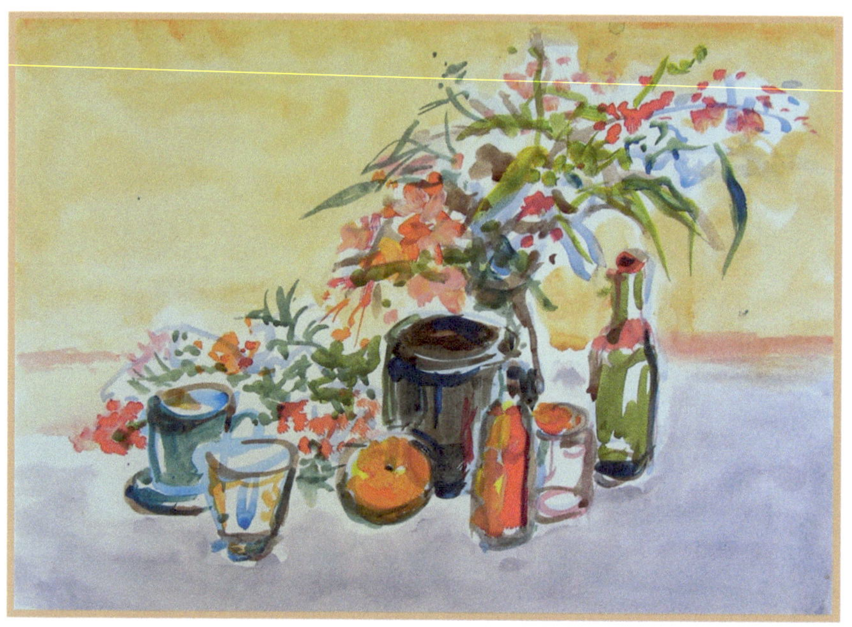

On the Table

Watercolour on paper, 28 x 37 cm, 2006

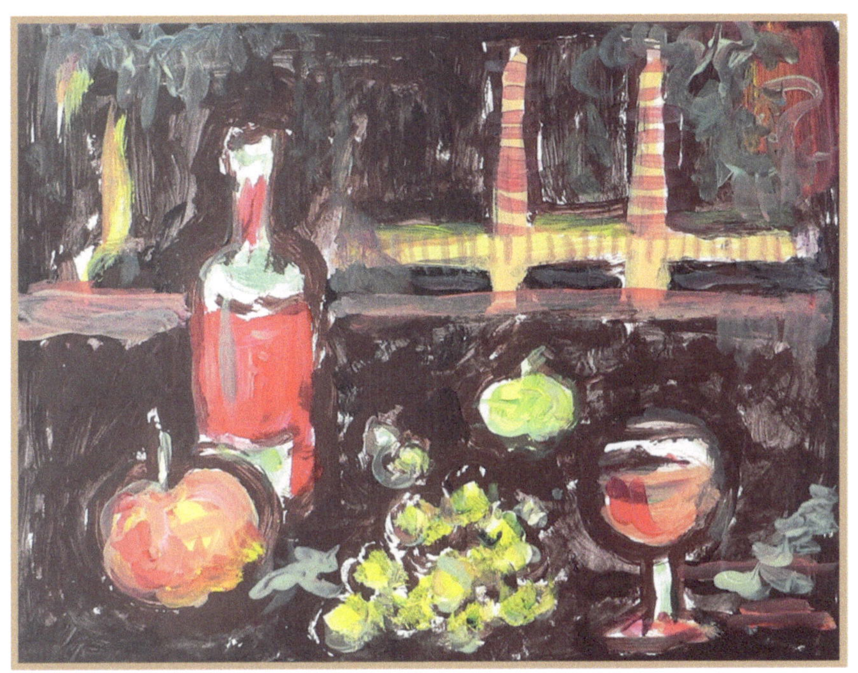

Still Life

Acrylic on paper, 23 x 29 cm, 2006

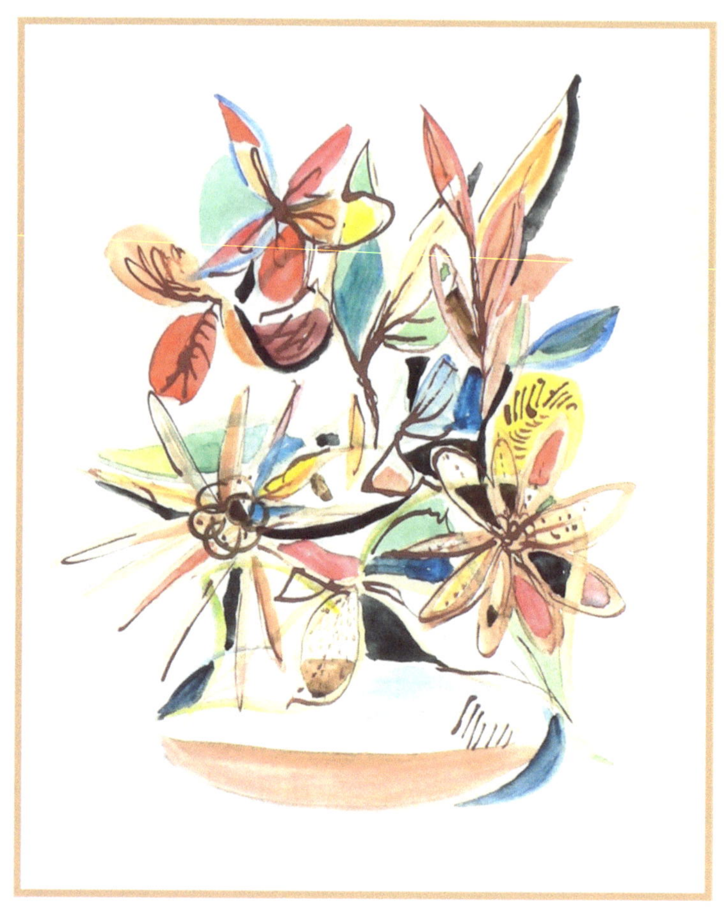

Flowers in a Vase

Watercolour on paper, 33 x 26 cm, 1980

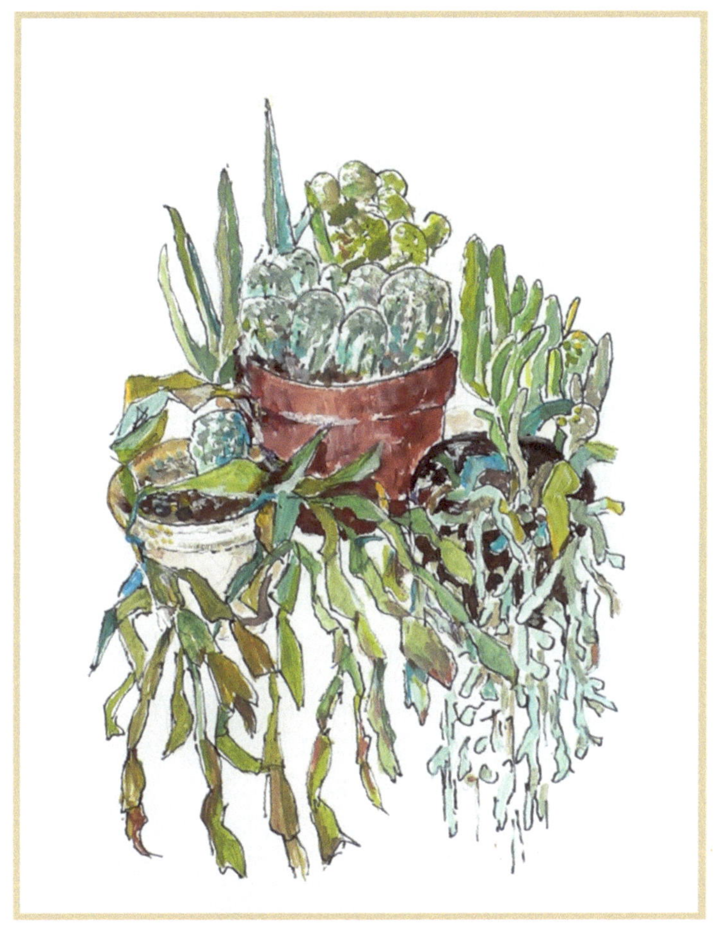

Cactacae

Acrylic and pen on paper, 34 x 25 cm, 2003

Mother Nature can change any and all plans.
(Unknown)

Nature gives to every time and season
some beauties of its own.
(Charles Dickens)

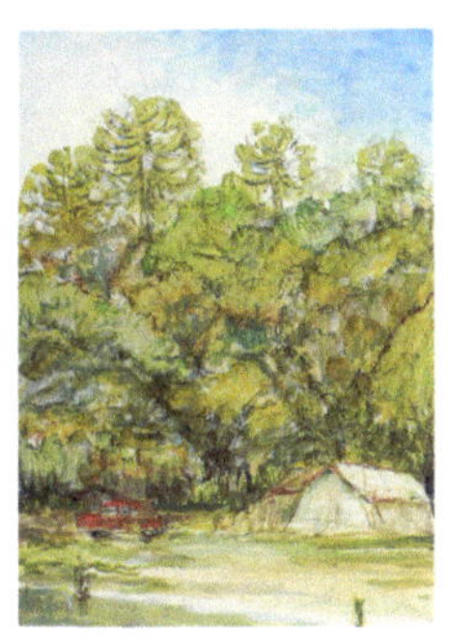

In the Country

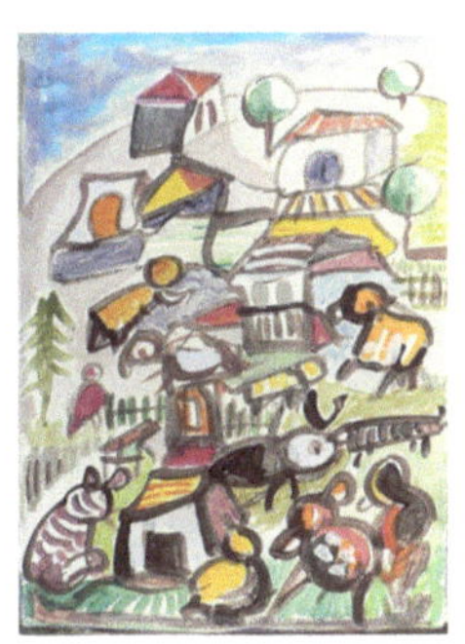

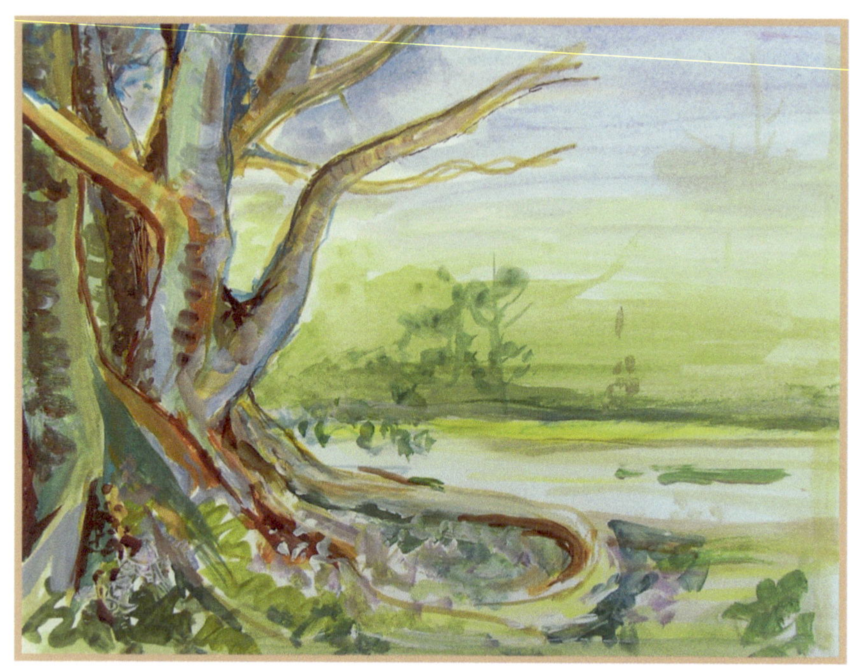

Tree by the Water

Acrylic on paper, 27 x 33 cm, 1986

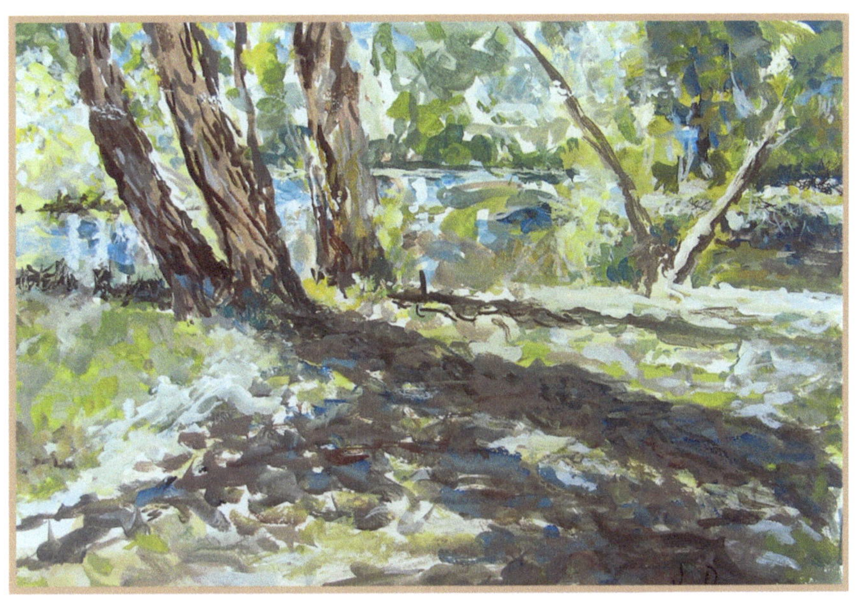

Hilliards Creek

Acrylic on paper, 27 x 38 cm, 2010

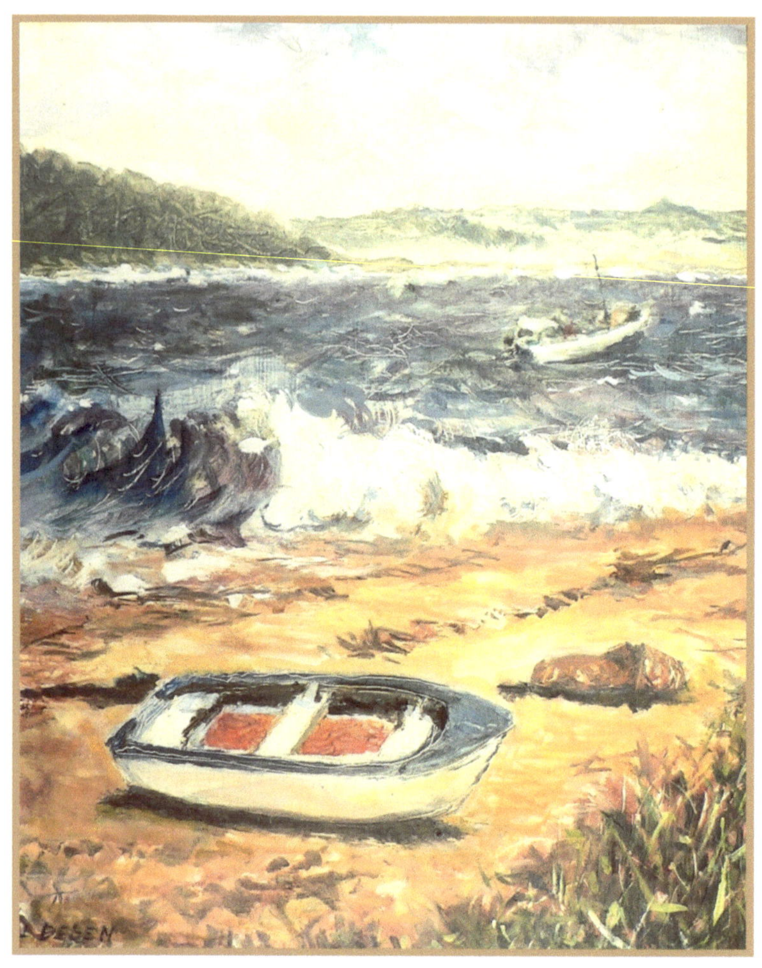

At the Sea

Oil on board, 40 x 30 cm, 1985

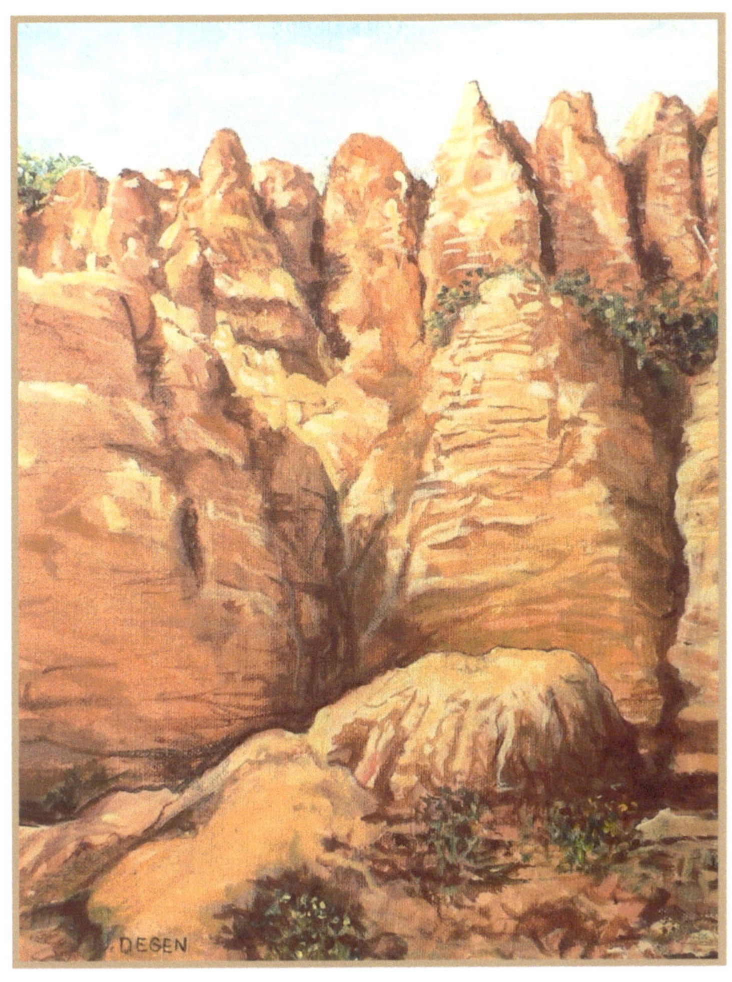

Rocks at the Seaside

Oil on canvas, 40 x 30 cm, 1989

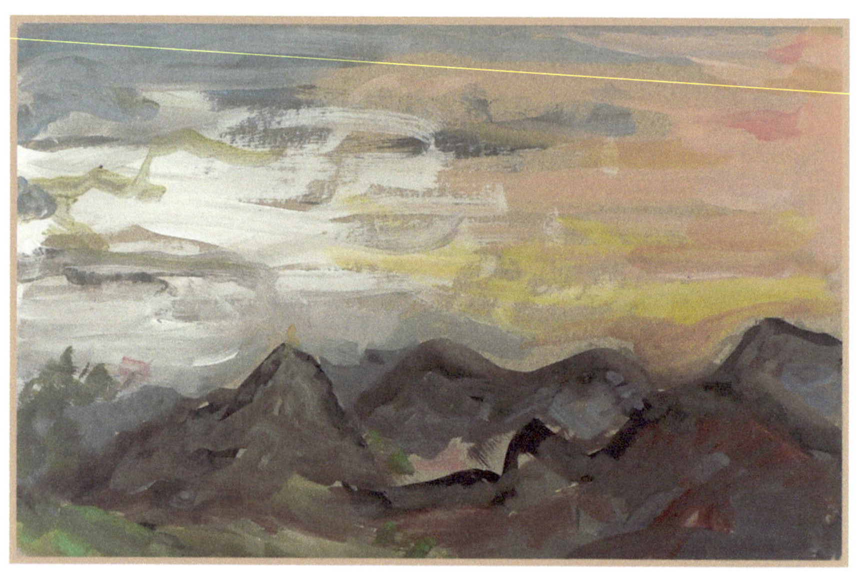

Changing Weather

Acrylic on paper, 19 x 29 cm, 2007

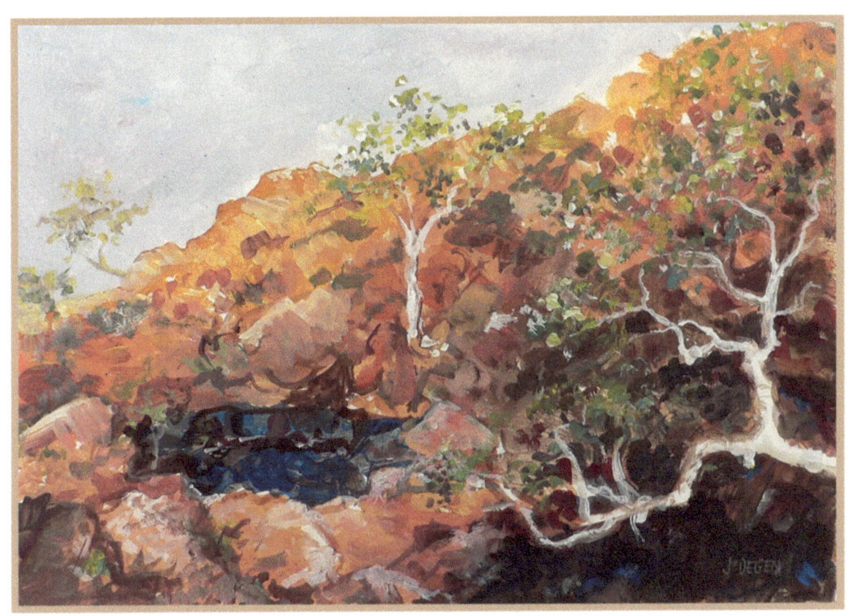

Bushy Hill

Acrylic on paper, 27 x 36 cm, 1998

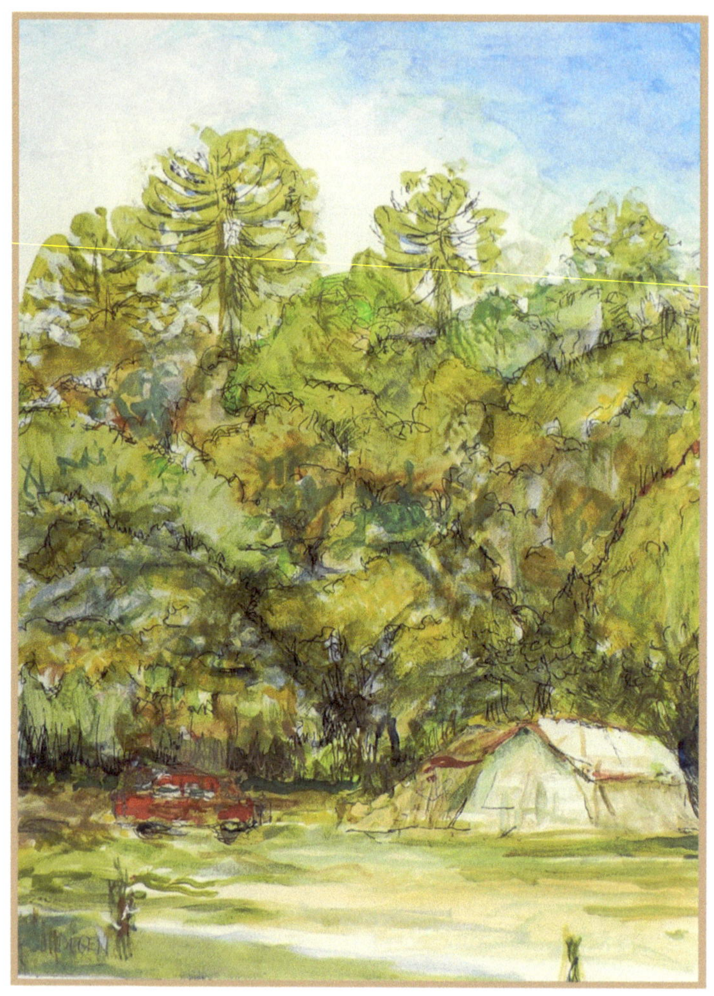

At Bunya Mountains

Acrylic and pen on paper, 39 x 28 cm, 2003

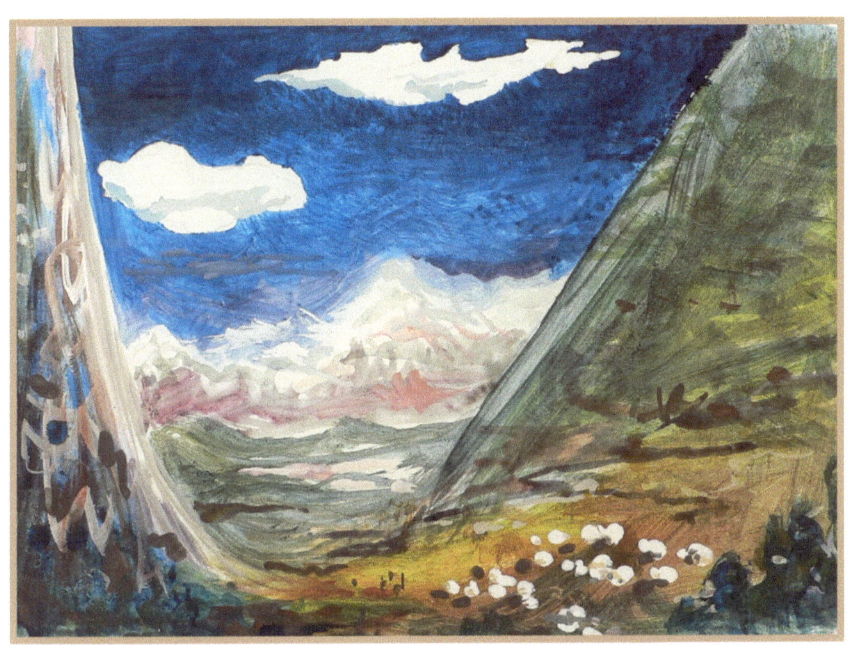

Memory of New Zealand

Acrylic on board, 26 x 36 cm, 2000

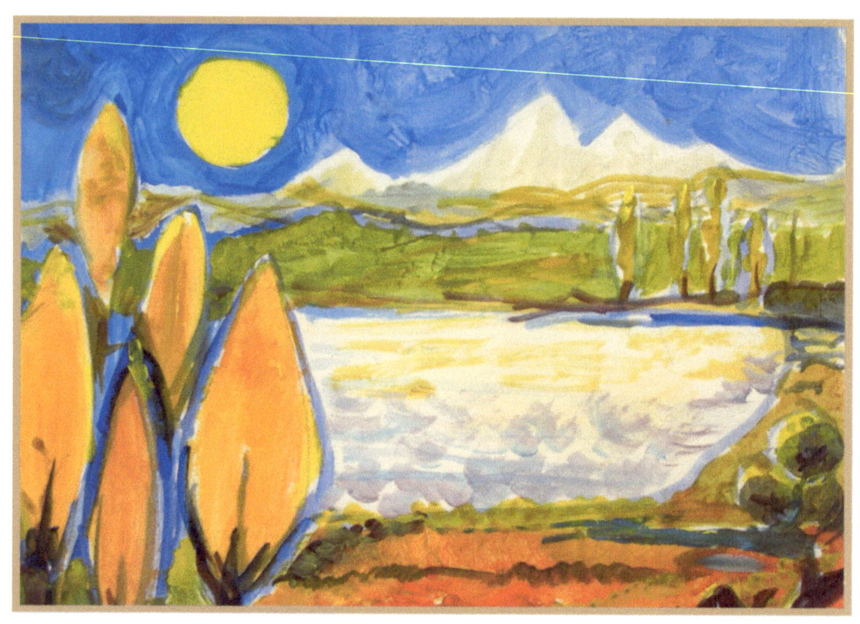

Sun Reclining

Acrylic on paper, 26 x 35 cm, 2008

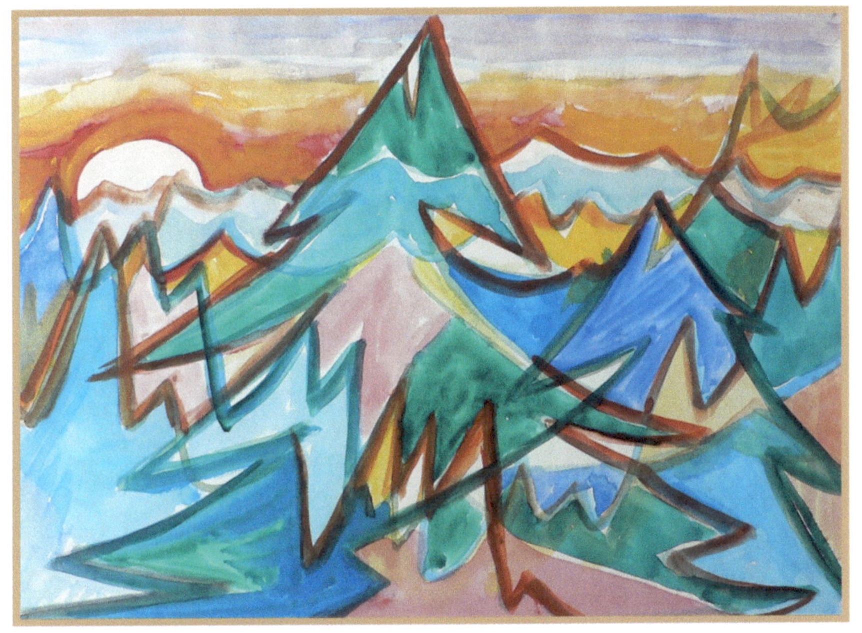

Rising Sun

Watercolour on paper, 27 x 36 cm, 2005

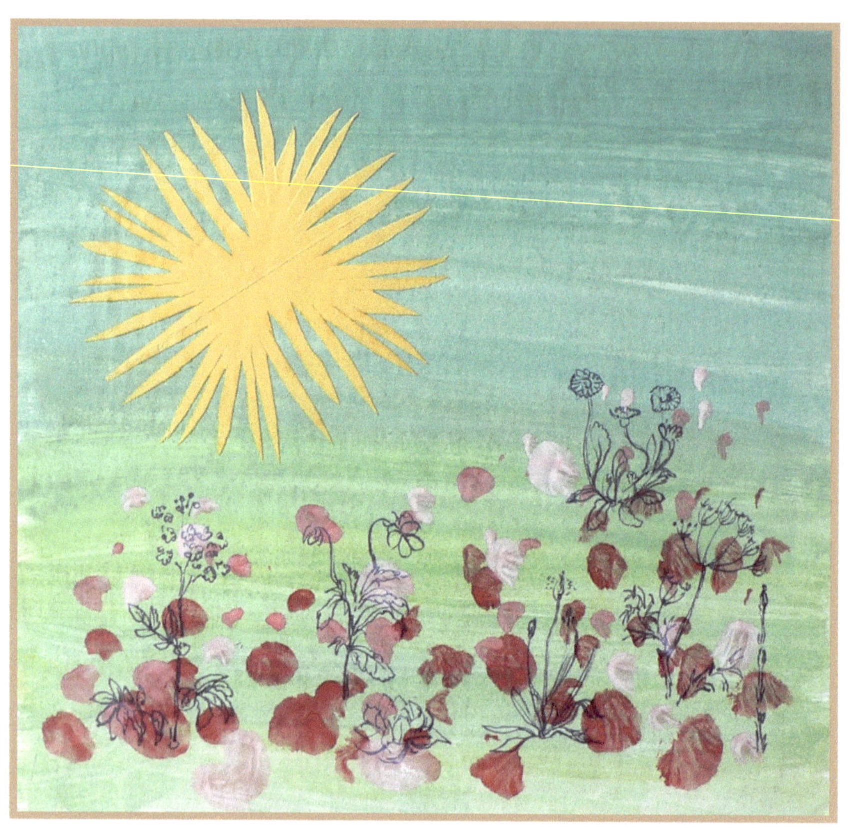

Sun in the Green

Mixed media on paper, 24 x 25 cm, 2003

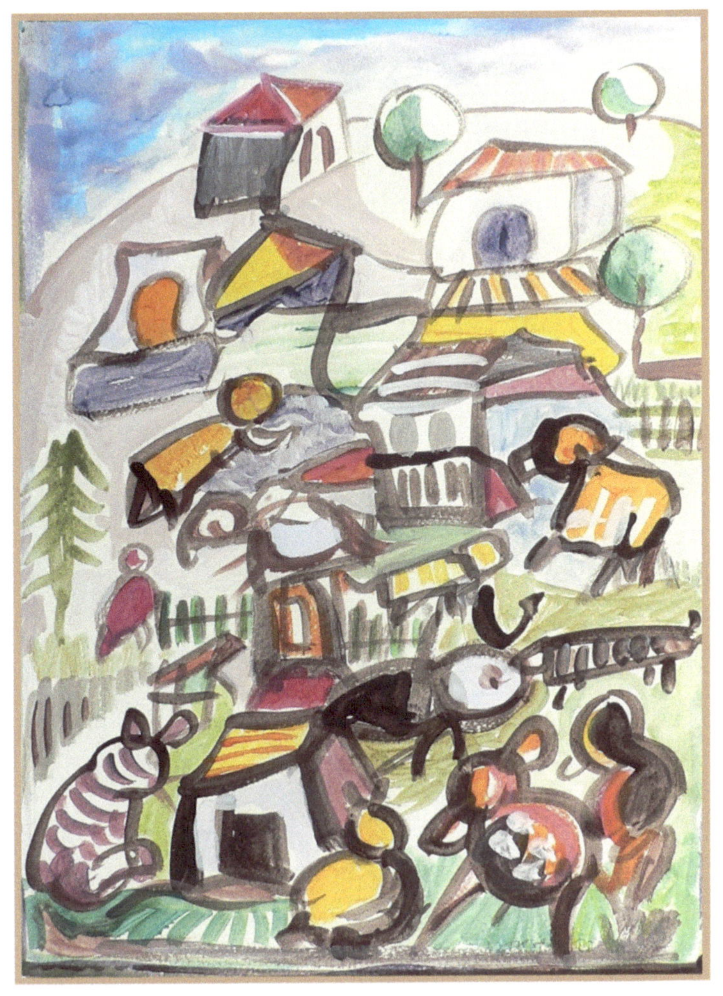

A Little Farm

Watercolour on paper, 34 x 24 cm, 2006

Water is the driving force in nature.
(Leonardo da Vinci)

For life and death are one,
even as the river and the sea are one.
(Khalil Gibran)

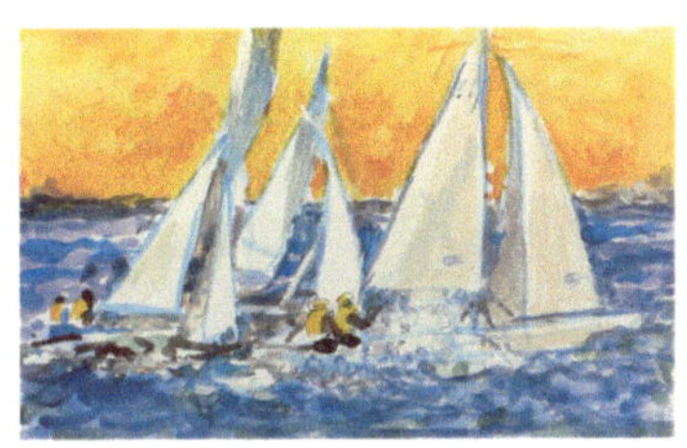

Sea and Water

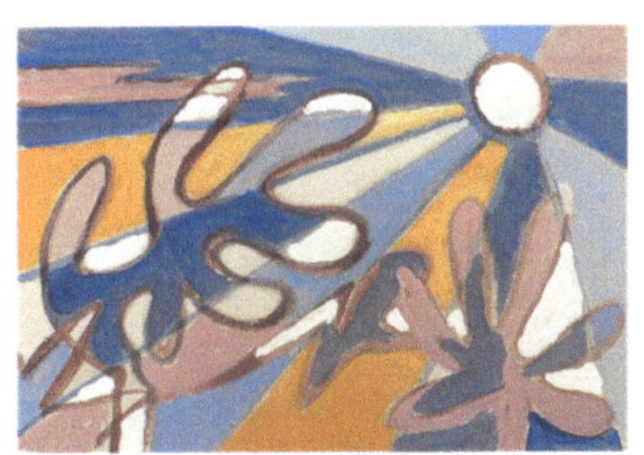

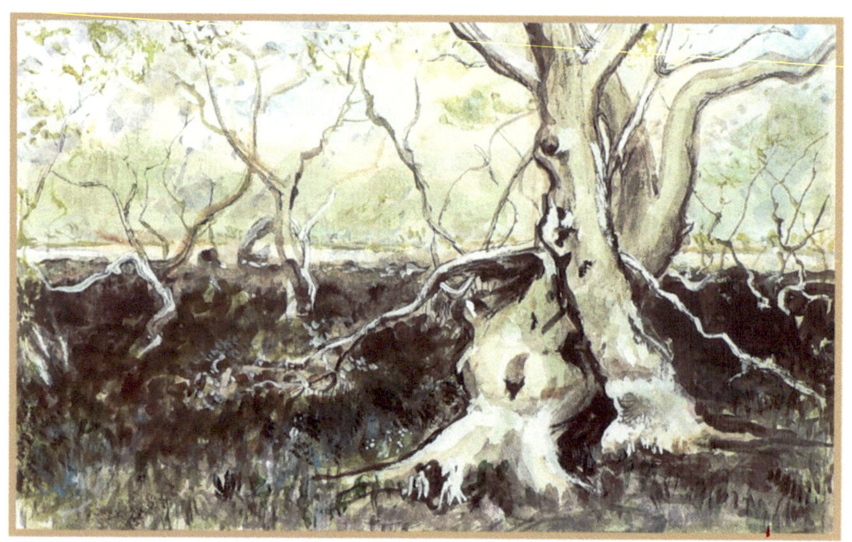

Wetlands

Watercolour on paper, 17 x 26 cm, 2003

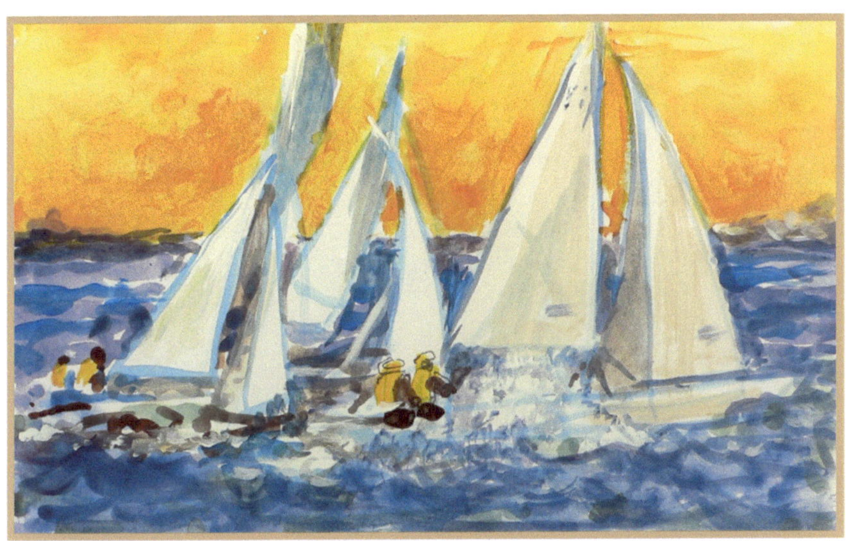

Regatta

Acrylic on paper, 18 x 28 cm, 2004

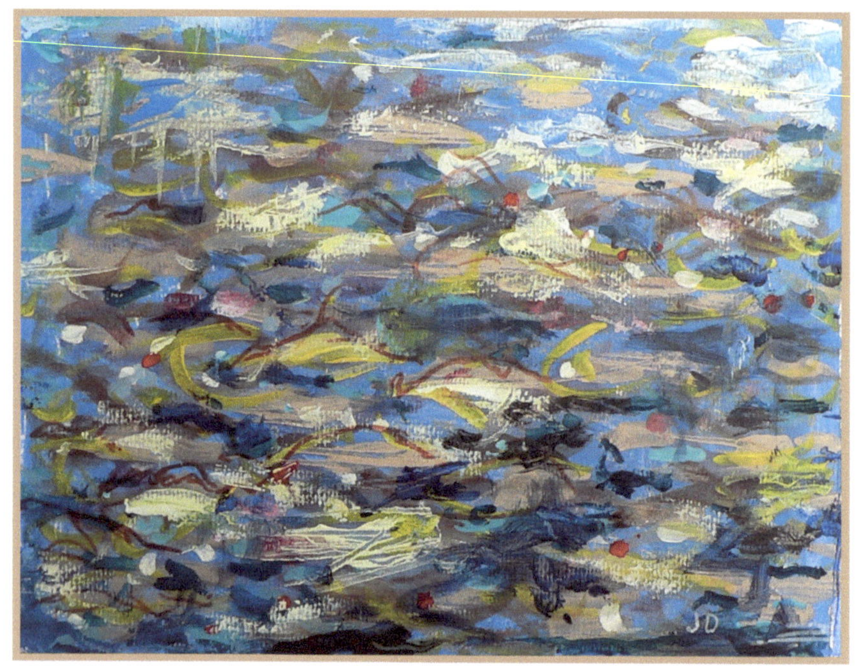

School in Progress

Mixed media on paper, 24 x 30 cm, 2008

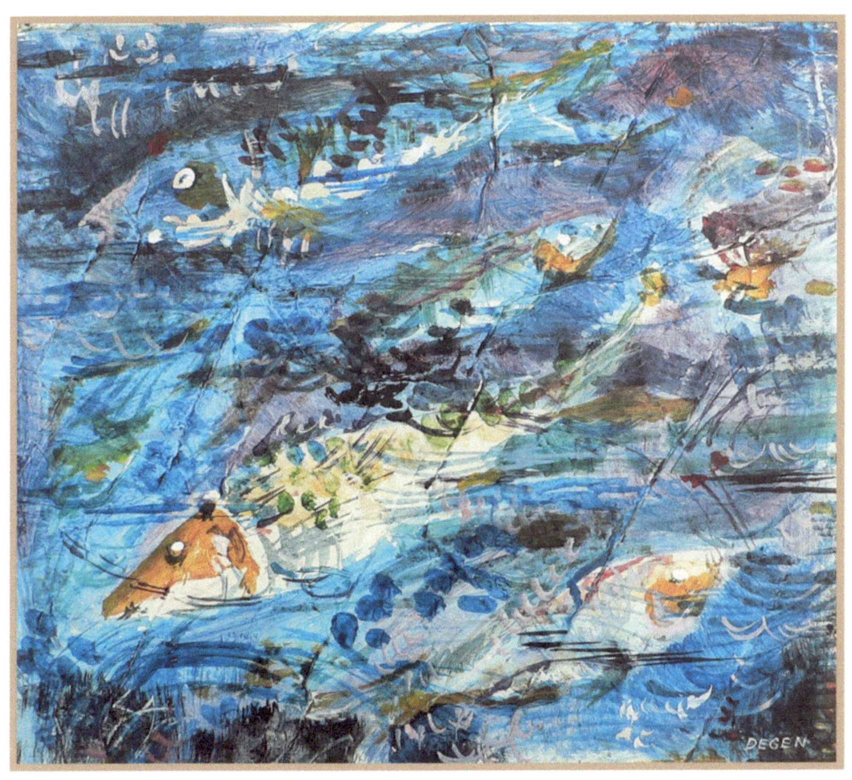

Blue Water

Acrylic on board, 33 x 36 cm, 1986

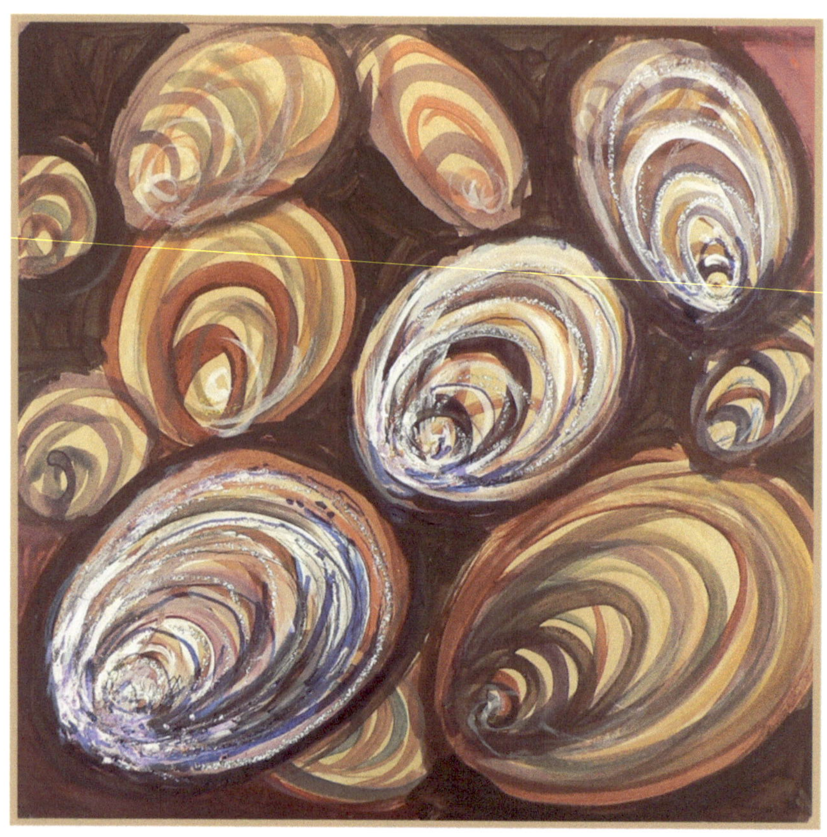

Shells

Mixed media on paper, 28 x 28 cm, 2005

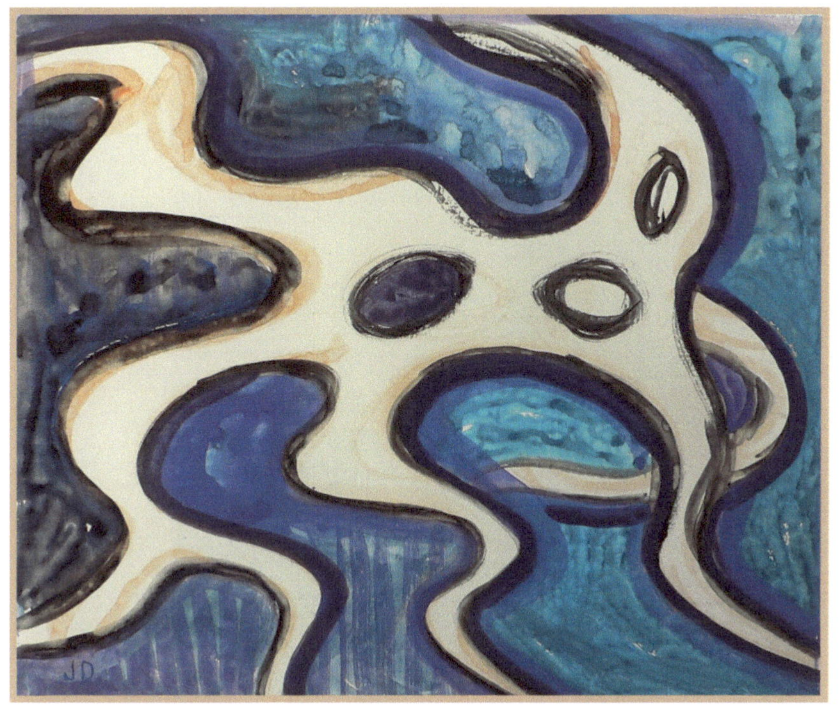

Octopus Blue

Gouache on board, 29 x 34 cm, 2006

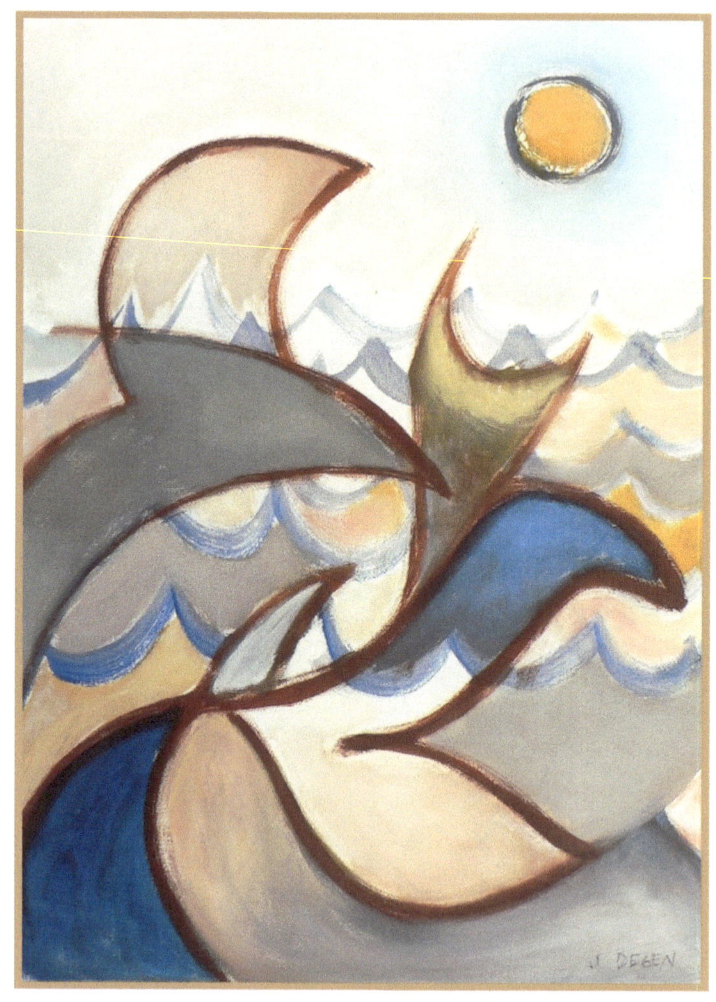

Big Waves

Oil on canvas, 42 x 30 cm, 2005

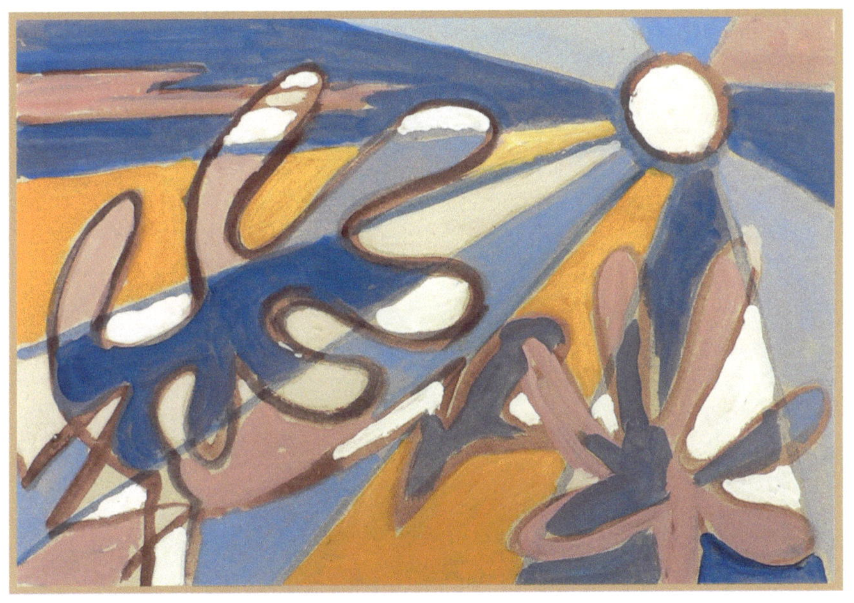

Leaves at the Sea

Gouache on board, 21 x 29 cm, 2003

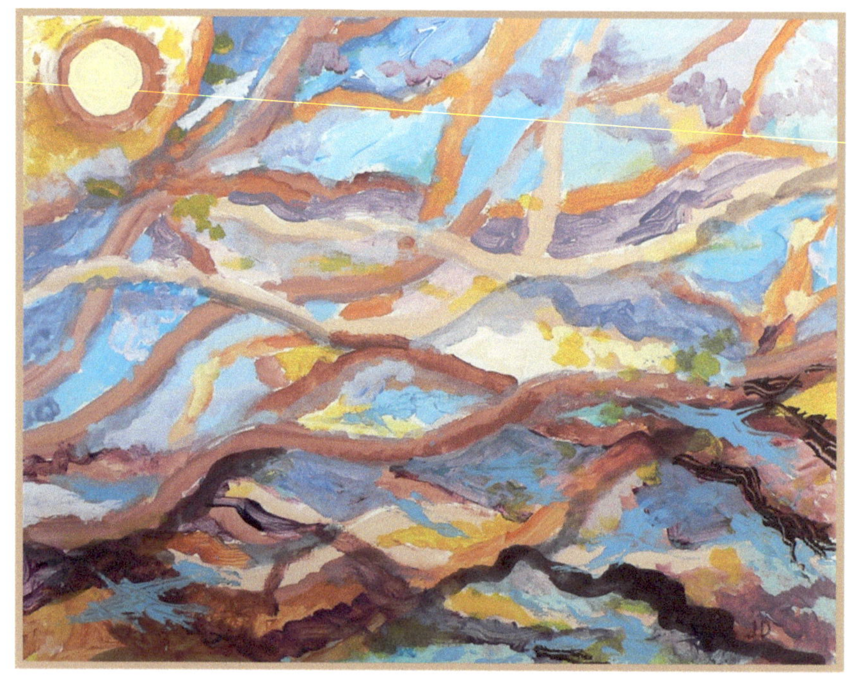

Stream Under Sun

Acrylic on board, 30 x 37 cm, 2009

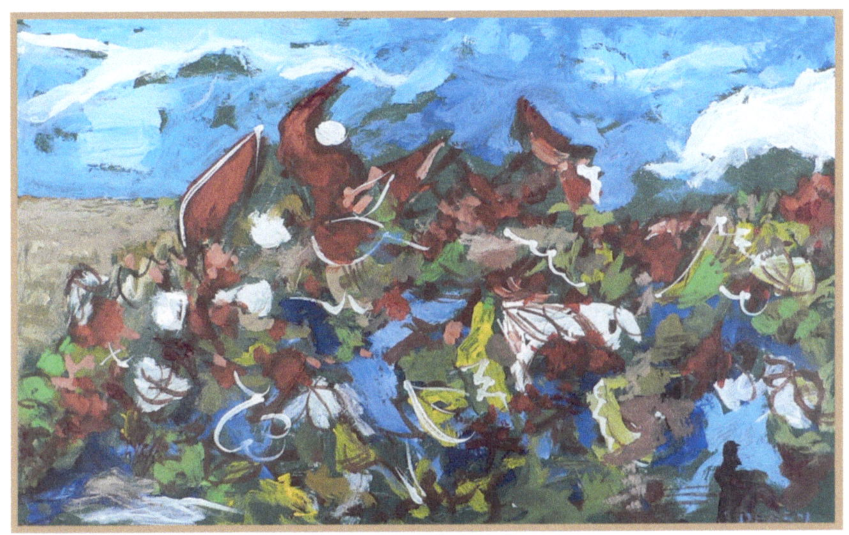

Close to Sea

Acrylic on board, 29 x 46 cm, 2011

The creation of a thousand forests is in one acorn.
(Unknown)

For in the true nature of things,
if we rightly consider,
every green tree is far more glorious
than if it were made of gold and silver.
(Martin Luther)

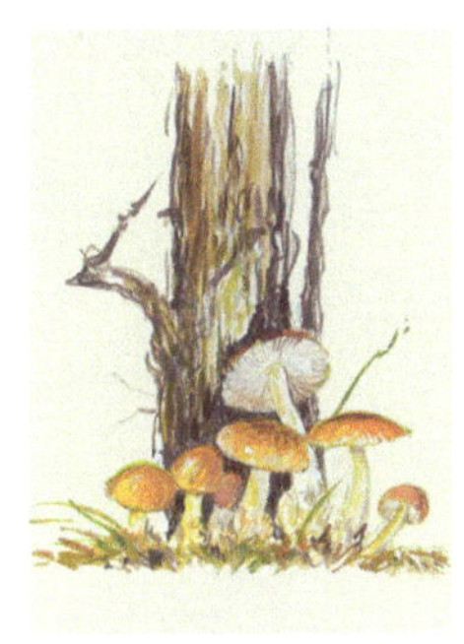

Trees and Plants

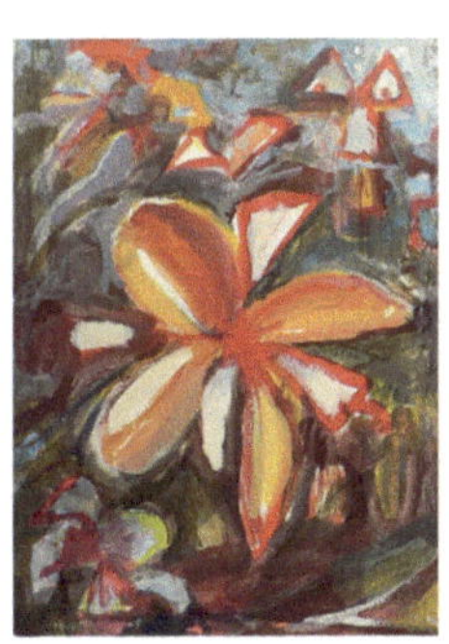

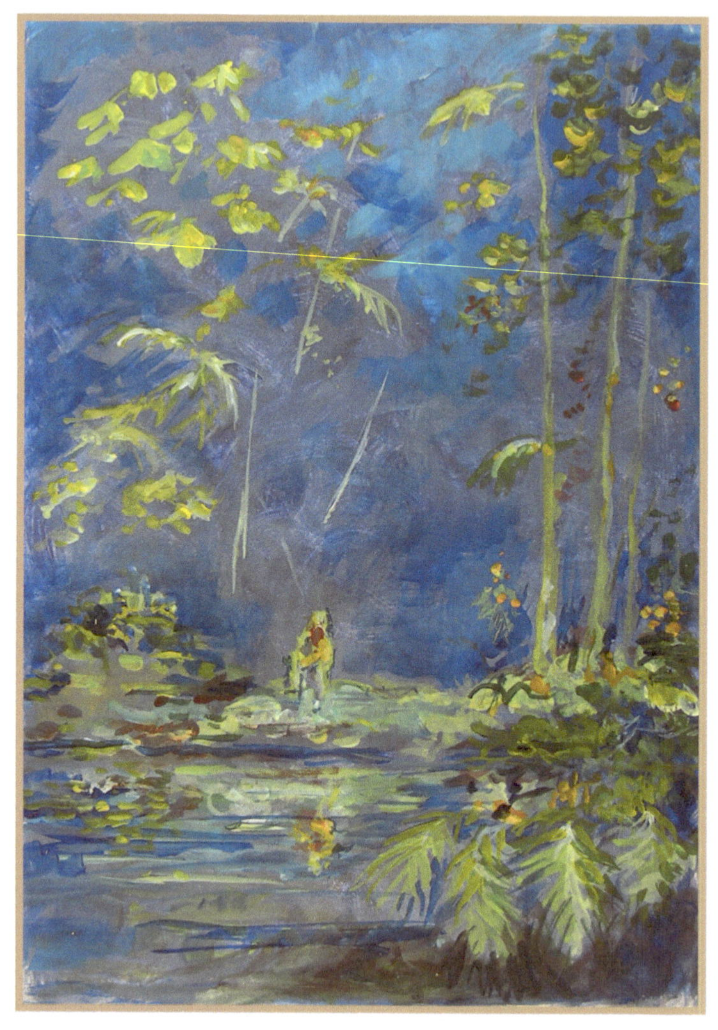

Dark Forest

Gouache on paper, 40 x 28 cm, 1984

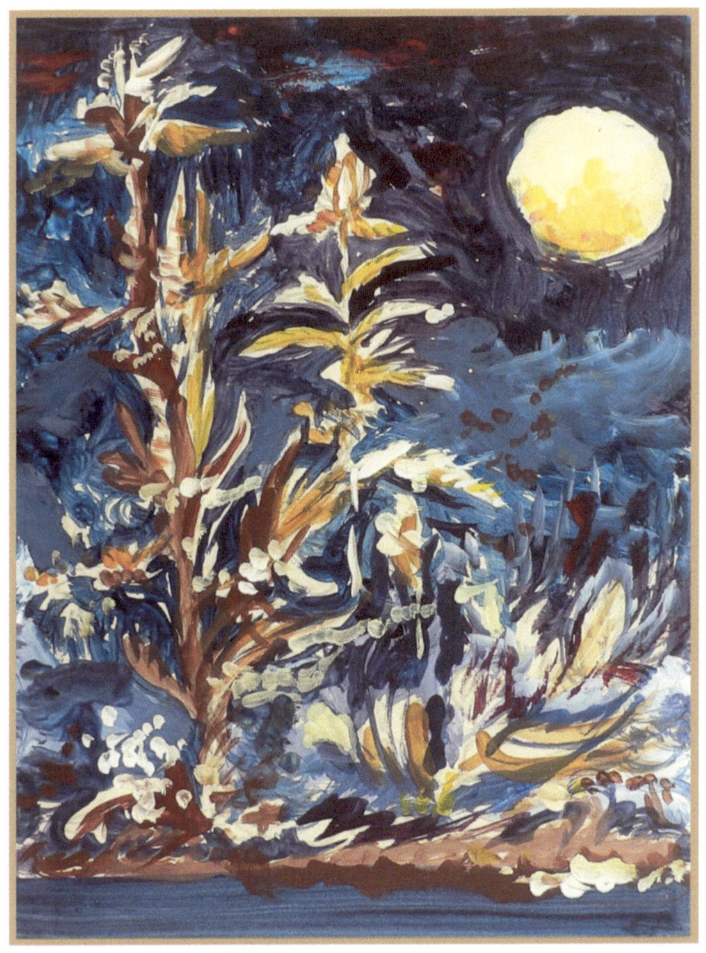

Night Scene

Gouache on paper, 33 x 24 cm, 1991

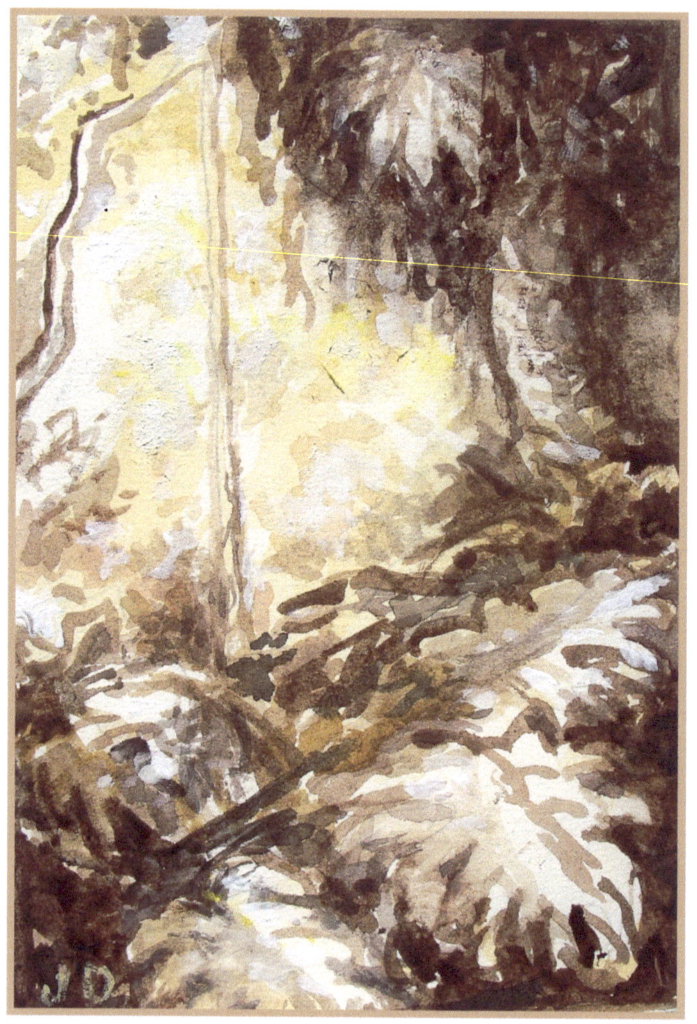

Sun in the Bush

Watercolour on paper, 20 x 14 cm, 2011

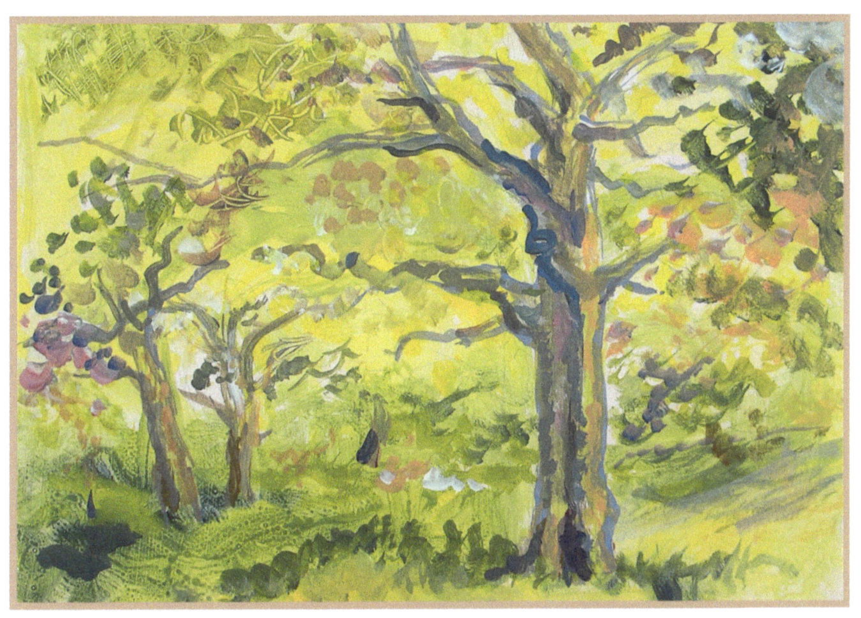

Trees in Yellow

Acrylic on paper, 26 x 35 cm, 2010

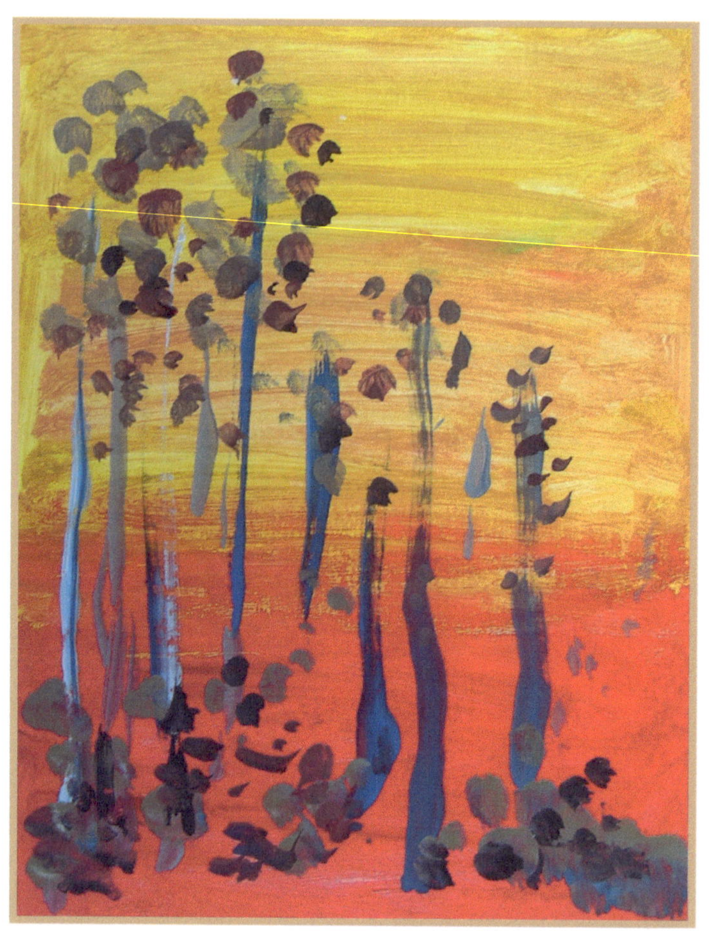

Trees

Acrylic on paper, 34 x 26 cm, 1986

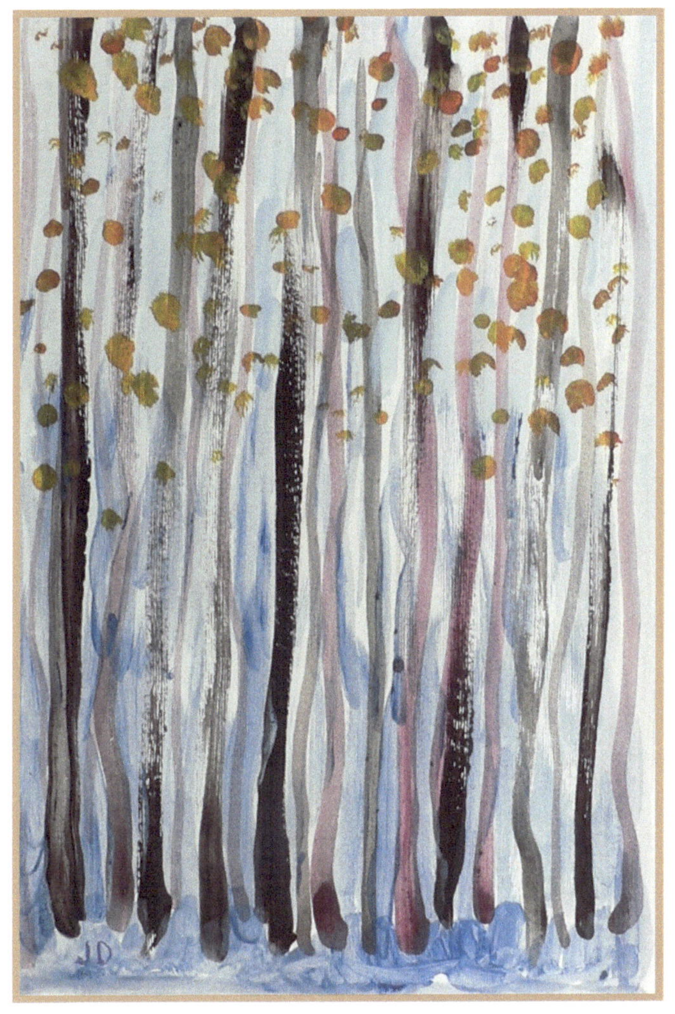

Late Autumn

Acrylic on paper, 31 x 20 cm, 2008

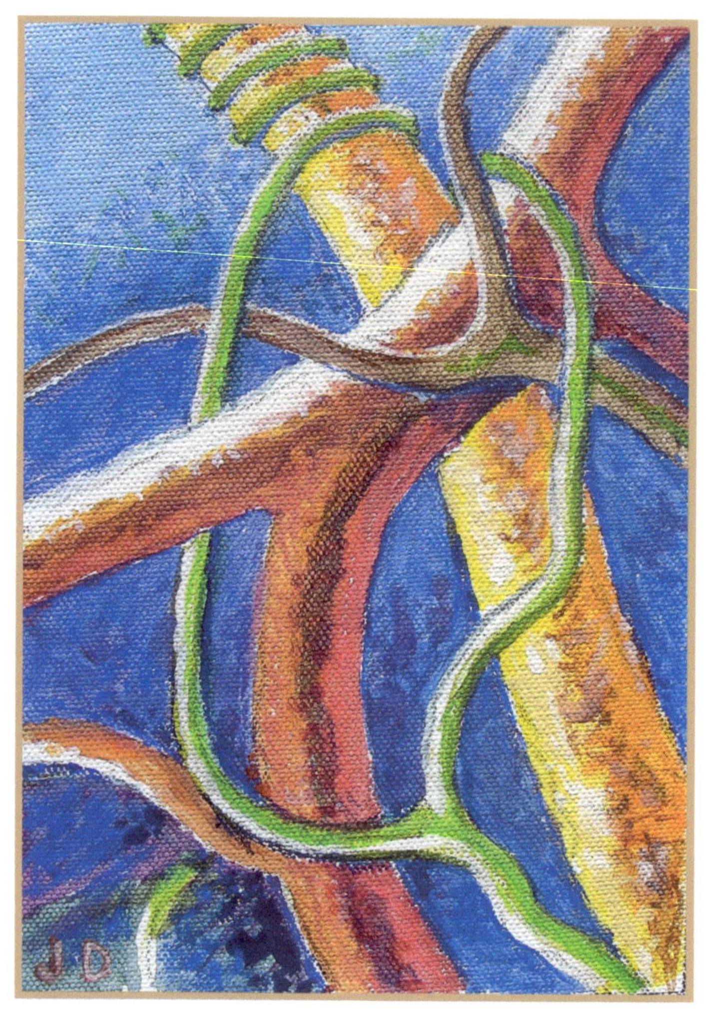

Embrace

Acrylic on canvas, 20 x 14 cm, 2011

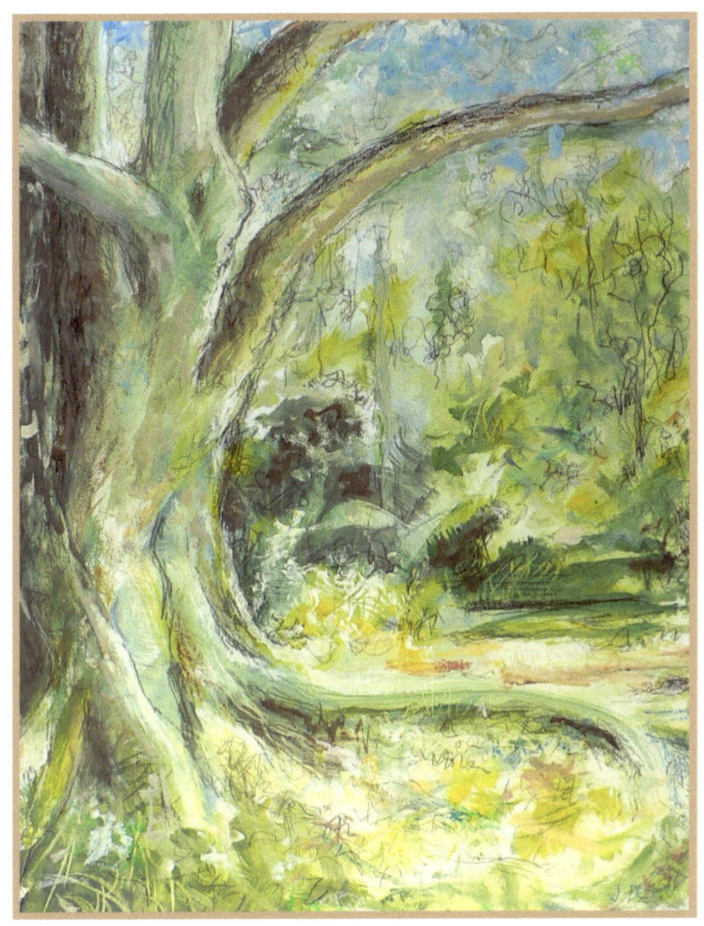

Sunny Bush

Oil on paper, 38 x 28 cm, 2006

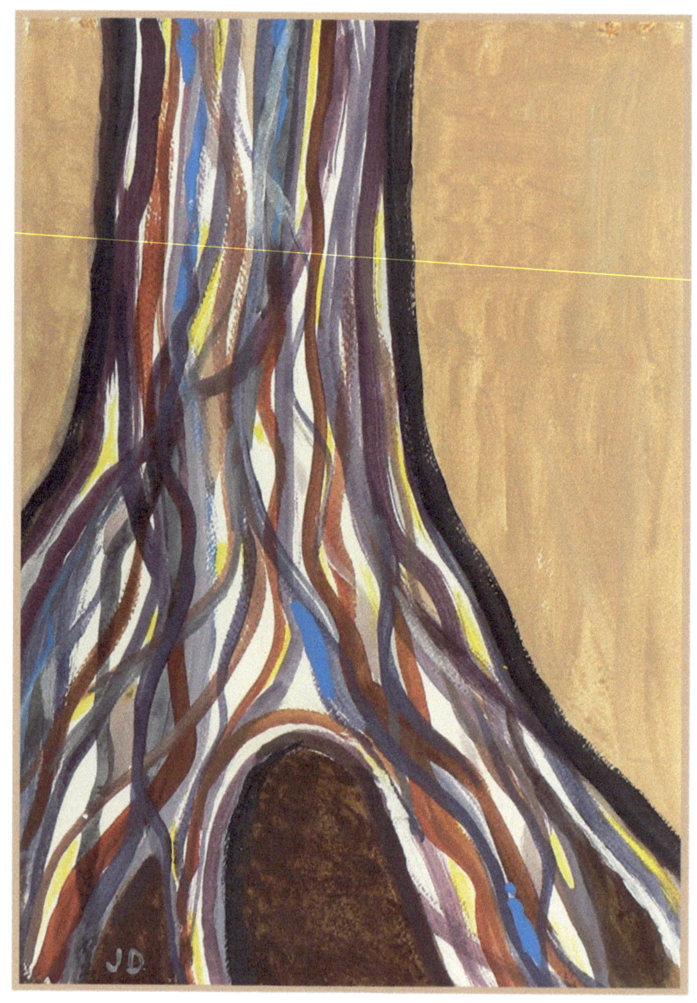

Hiding Place

Acrylic on paper, 42 x 29 cm, 2008

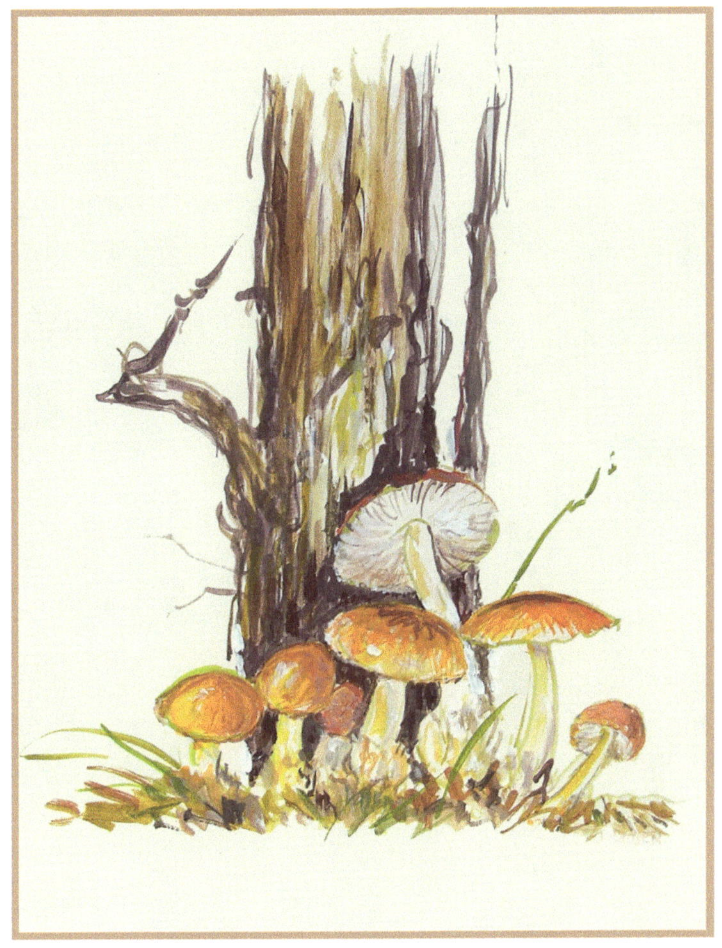

Mushrooms

Gouache on paper, 33 x 25 cm, 2003

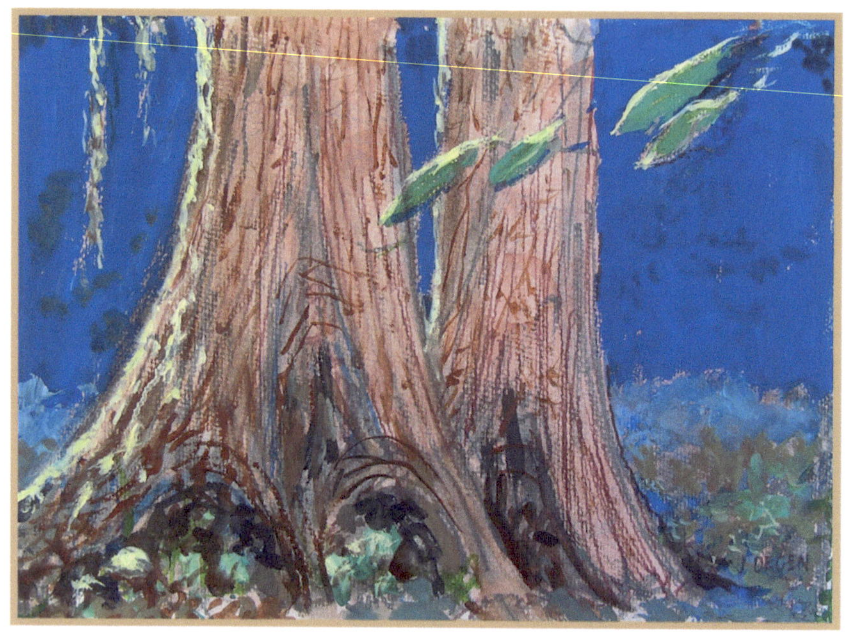

Two Trees

Mixed media on paper, 27 x 36 cm, 2010

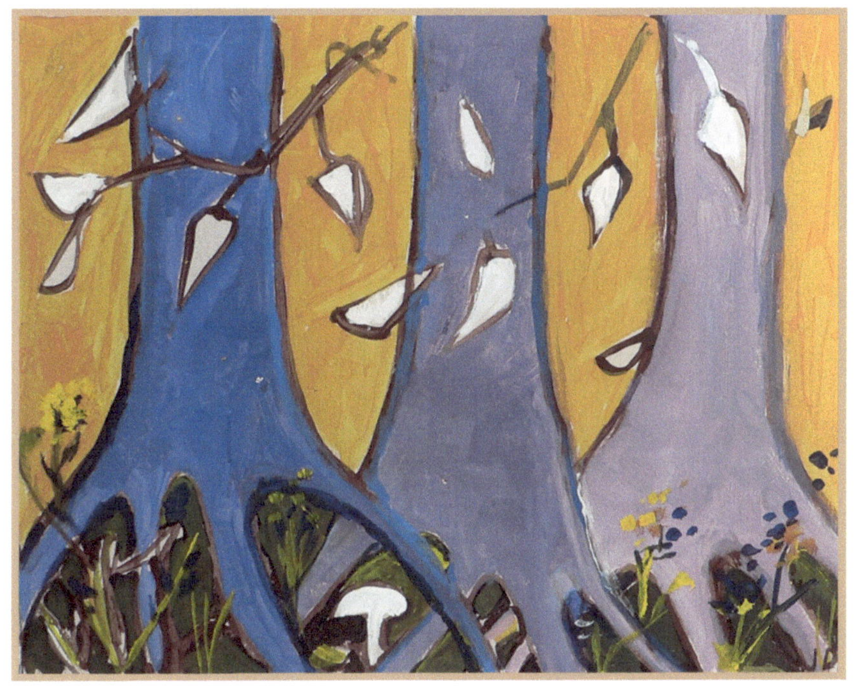

Moody Forest

Acrylic on paper, 16 x 32 cm, 2008

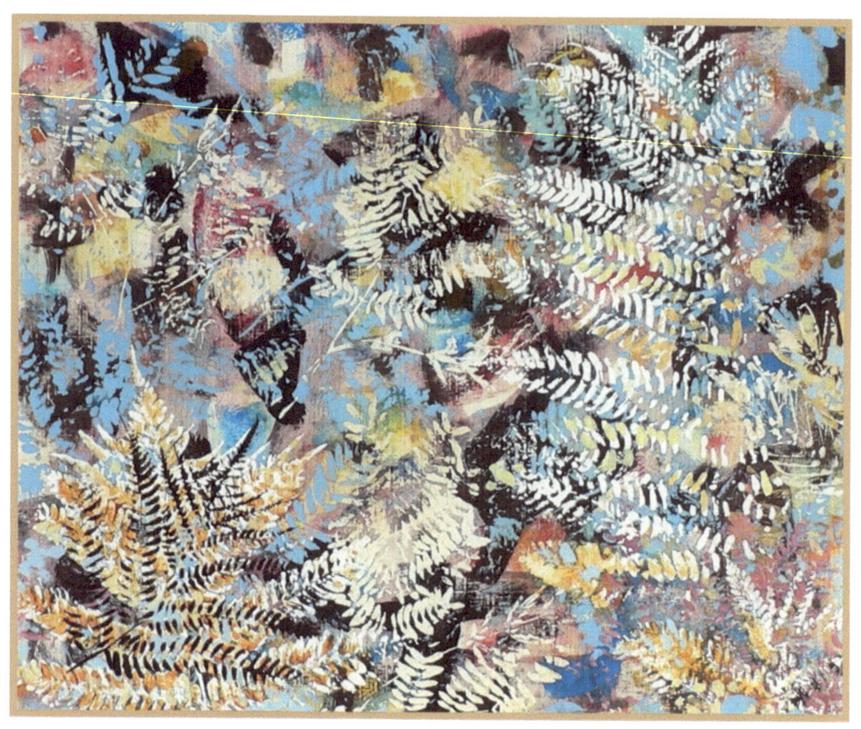

Heath

Acrylic print on paper, 36 x 43 cm, 2005

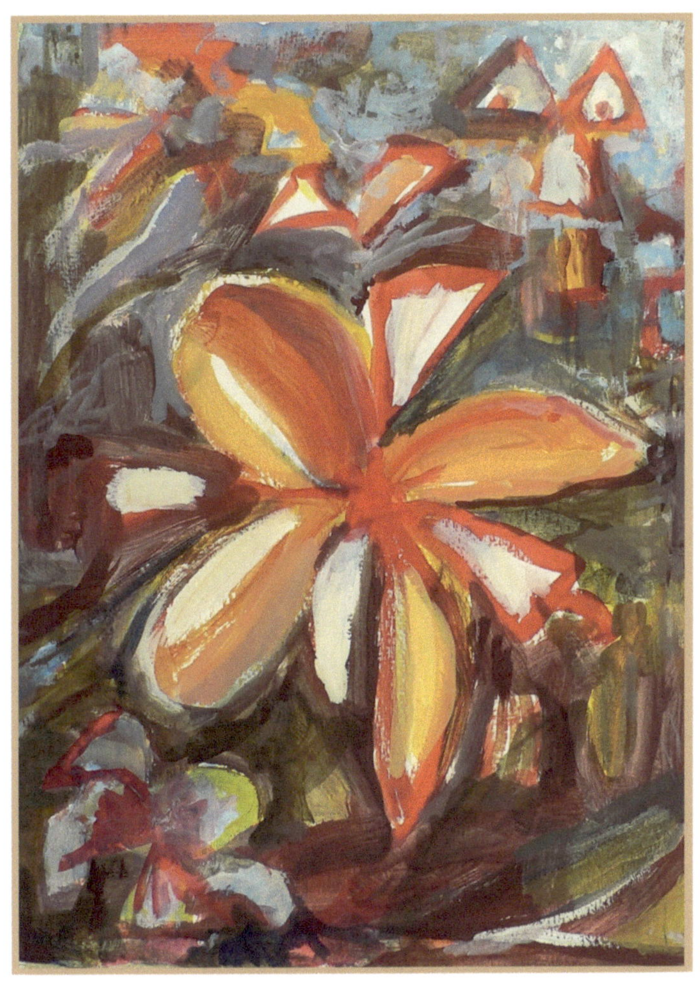

Wild Grove

Acrylic on paper, 39 x 28 cm, 2012

How beautifully leaves grow old.
How full of light and color are their last days.
(George Burns)

If one really loves nature,
one can find beauty everywhere.
(Vincent van Gogh)

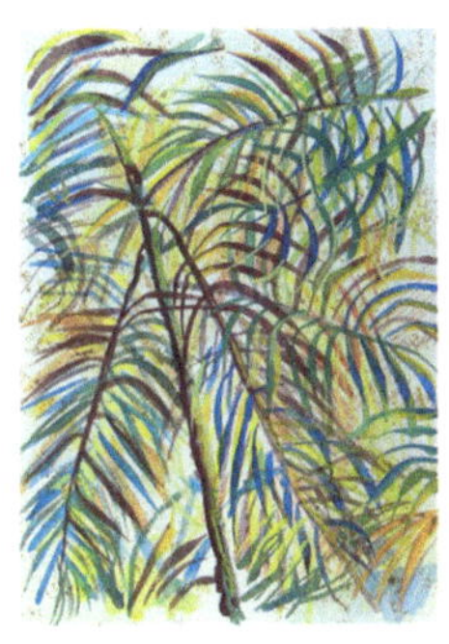

Leafage

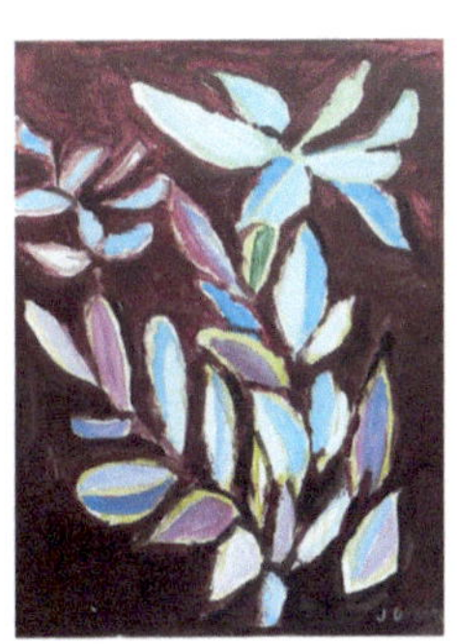

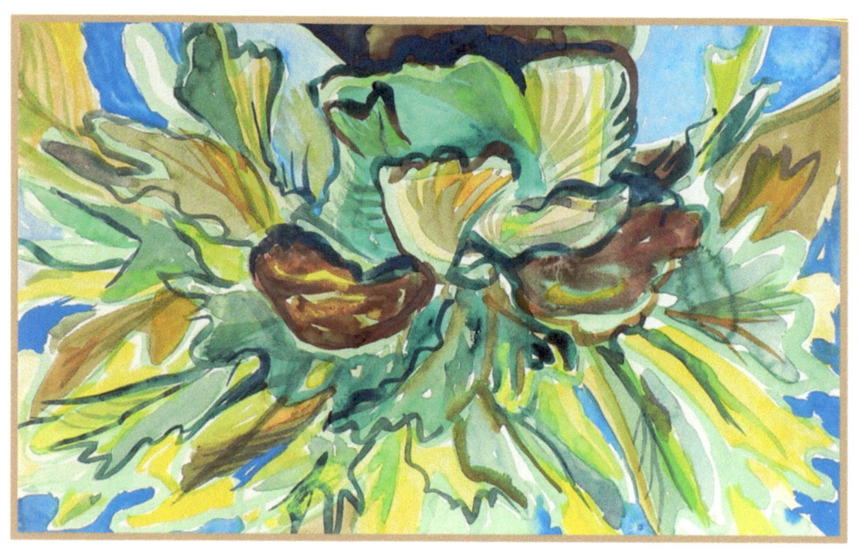

Platycerium Grande

Watercolour on paper, 25 x 37 cm, 1999

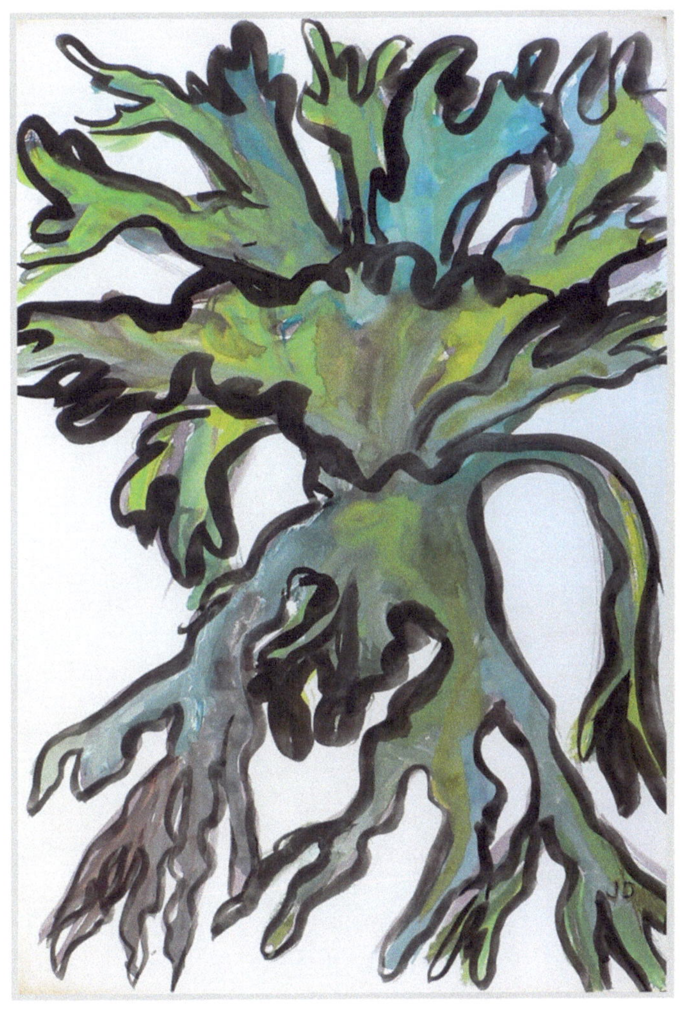

Hanging Greenery

Acrylic on paper, 37 x 25 cm, 2002

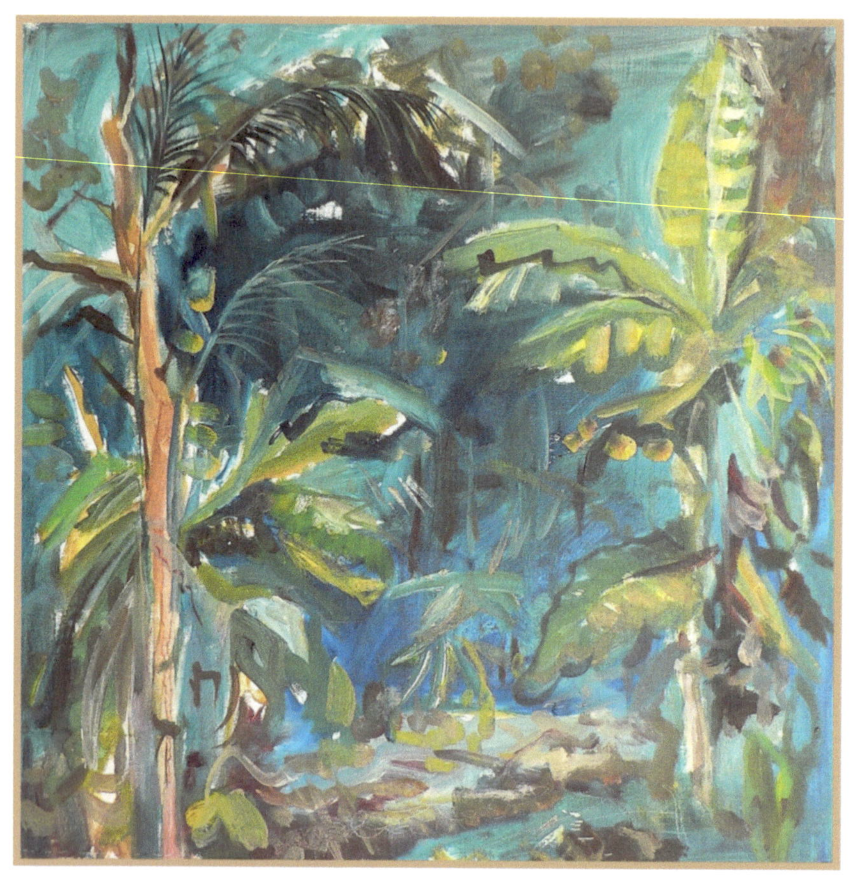

Palms

Oil on board, 32 x 27 cm, 2007

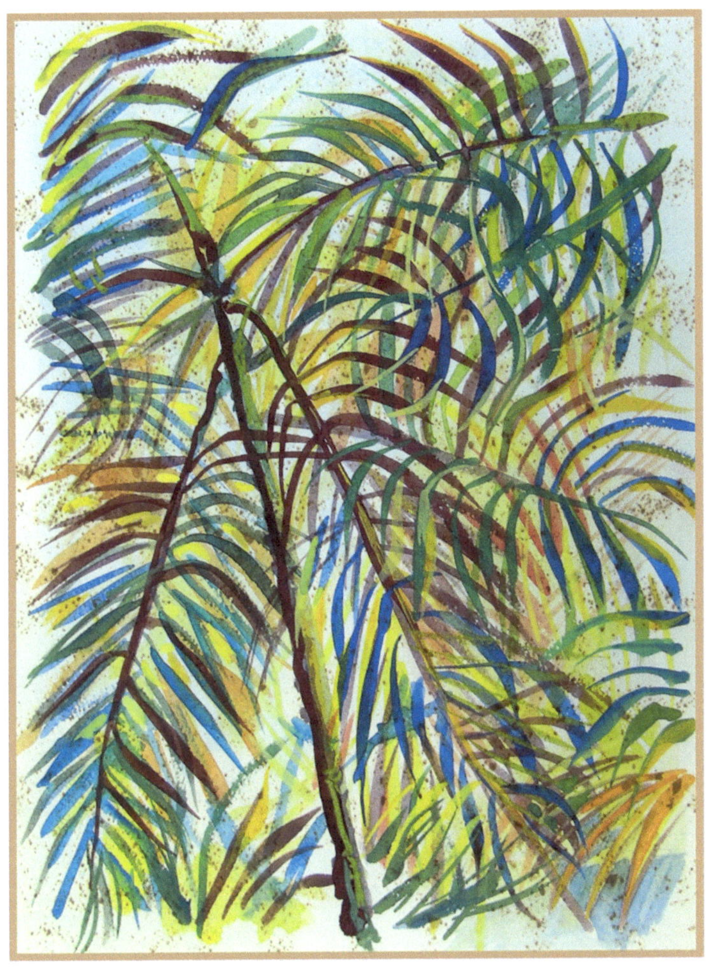

Palm Leaves

Gouache on paper, 37 x 26 cm, 2002

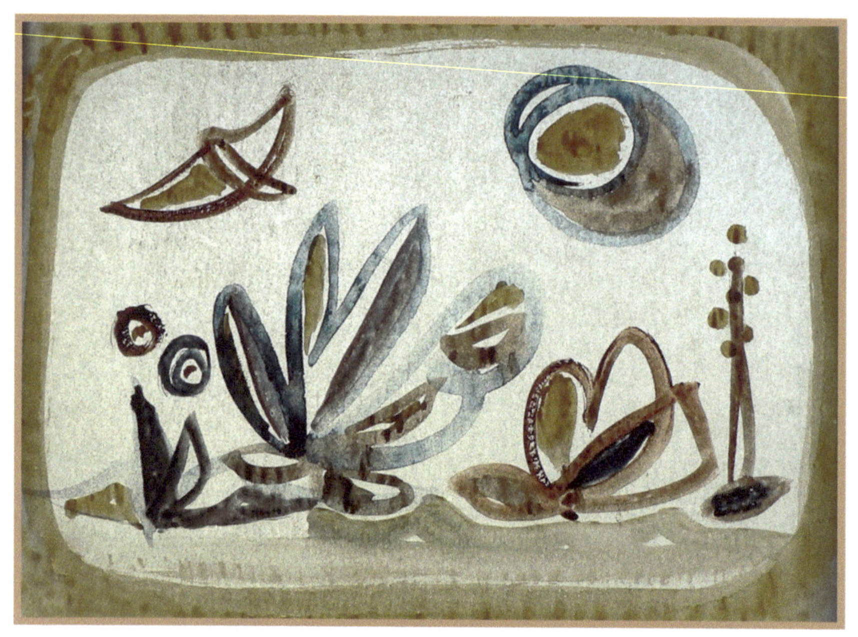

A Little Scene

Watercolour on paper, 23 x 29 cm, 2006

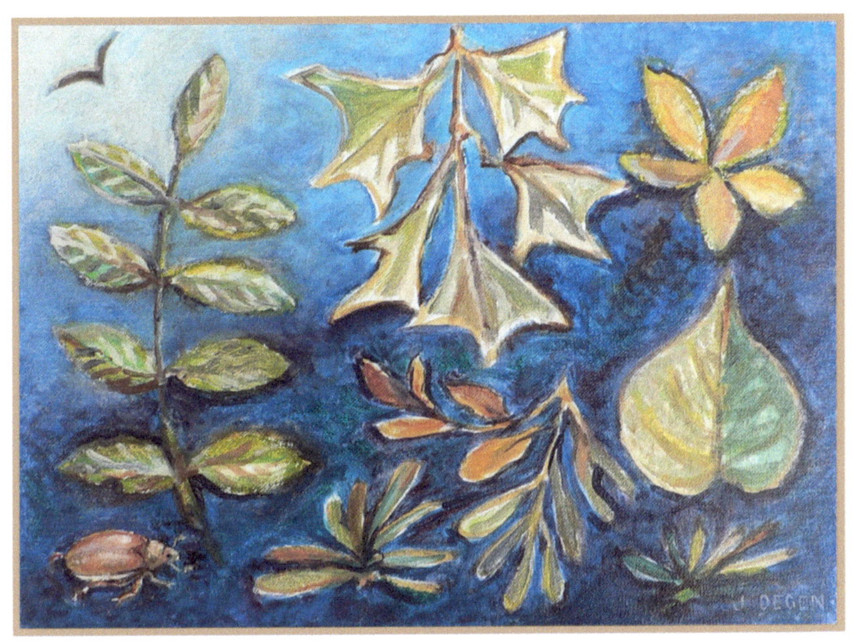

Botanical

Oil on board, 30 x 40 cm, 2001

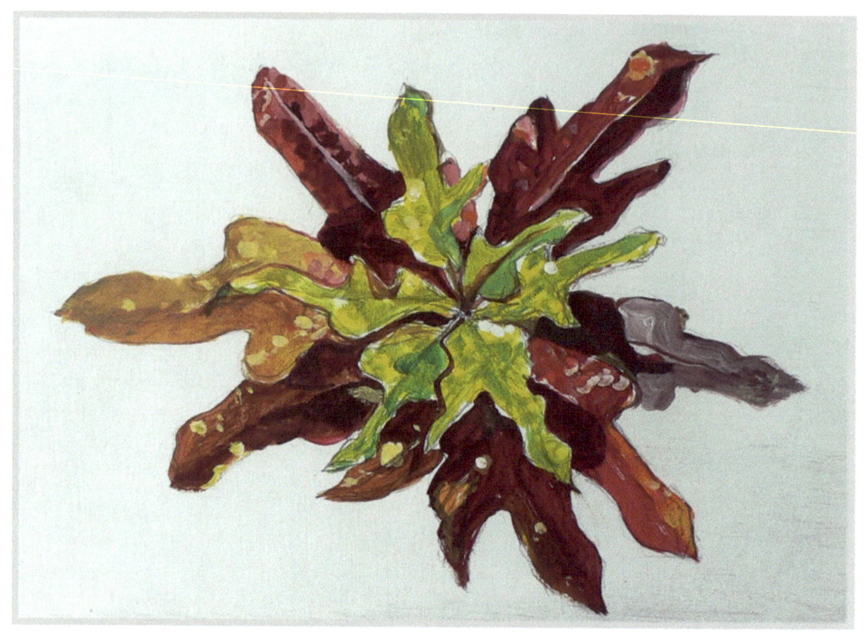

Colours Displayed

Acrylic on paper, 22 x 30 cm, 2008

69

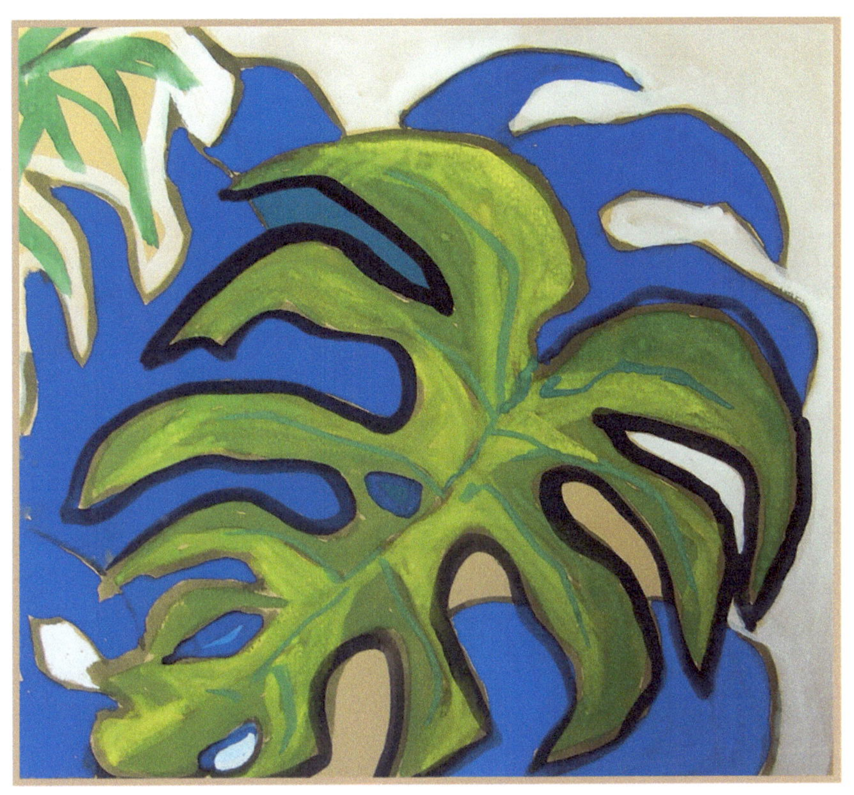

Big Leaf

Gouache on paper, 27 x 28 cm, 1985

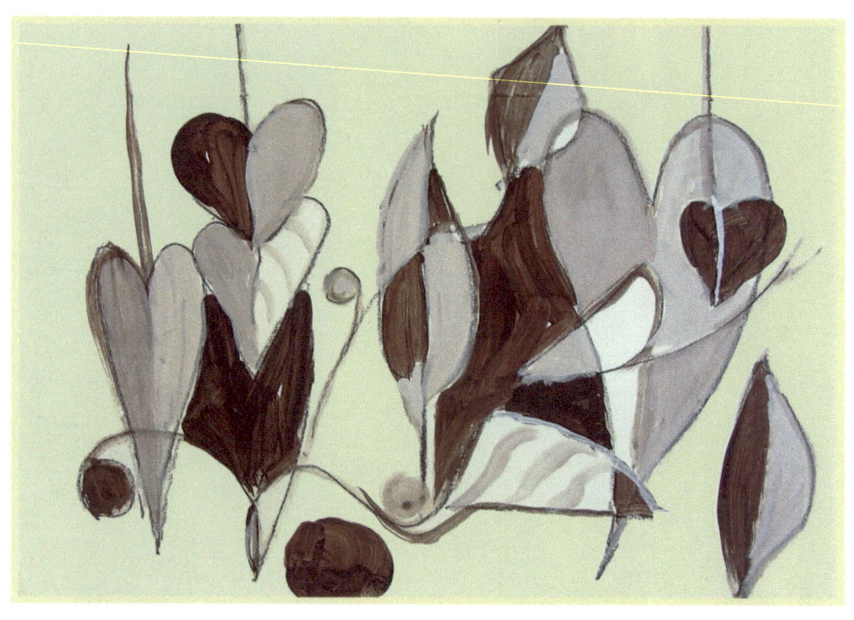

Leaves in the Air

Acrylic on paper, 24 x 33 cm, 2001

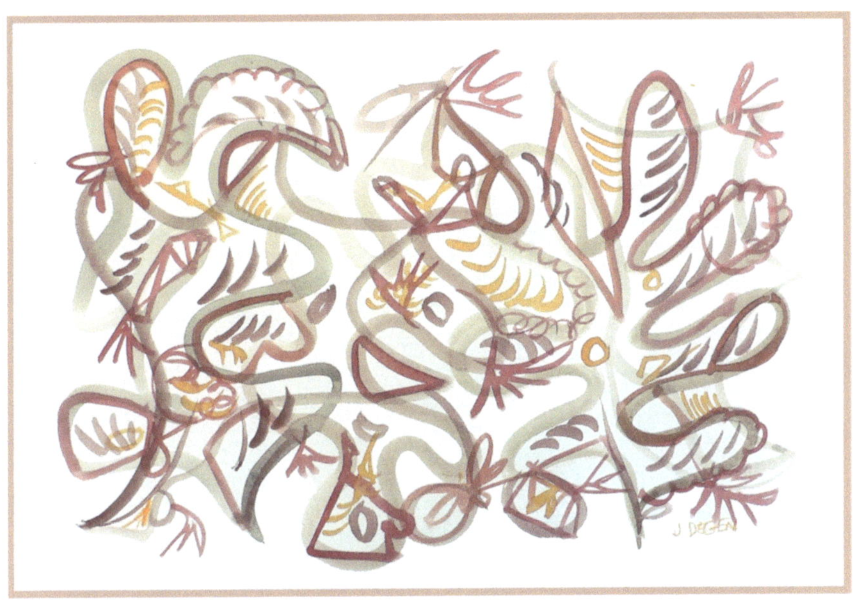

Leaves Aplenty

Watercolour on paper, 28 x 38 cm, 2004

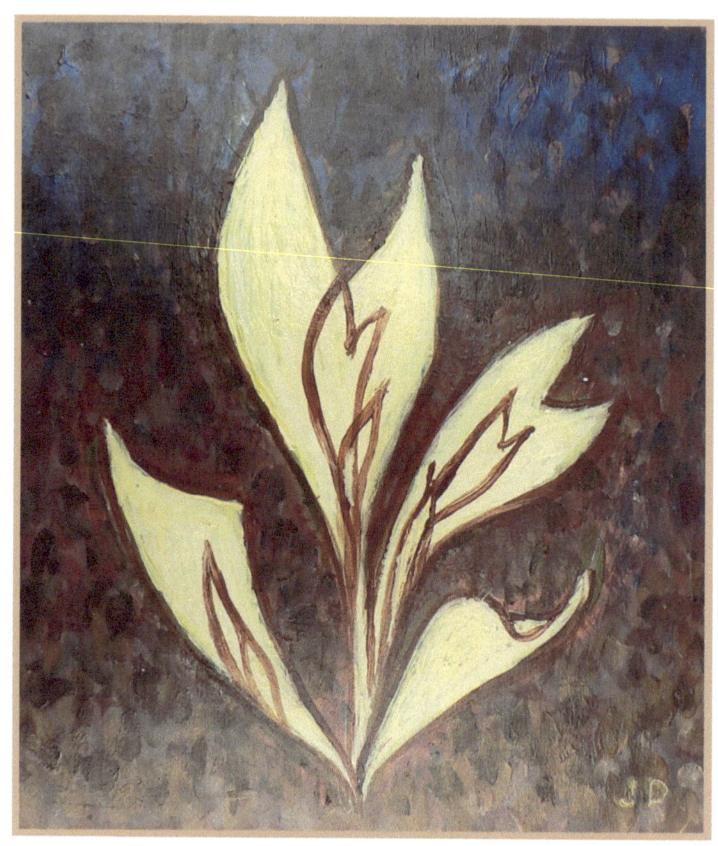

Leaves

Acrylic on board, 29 x 24 cm, 2012

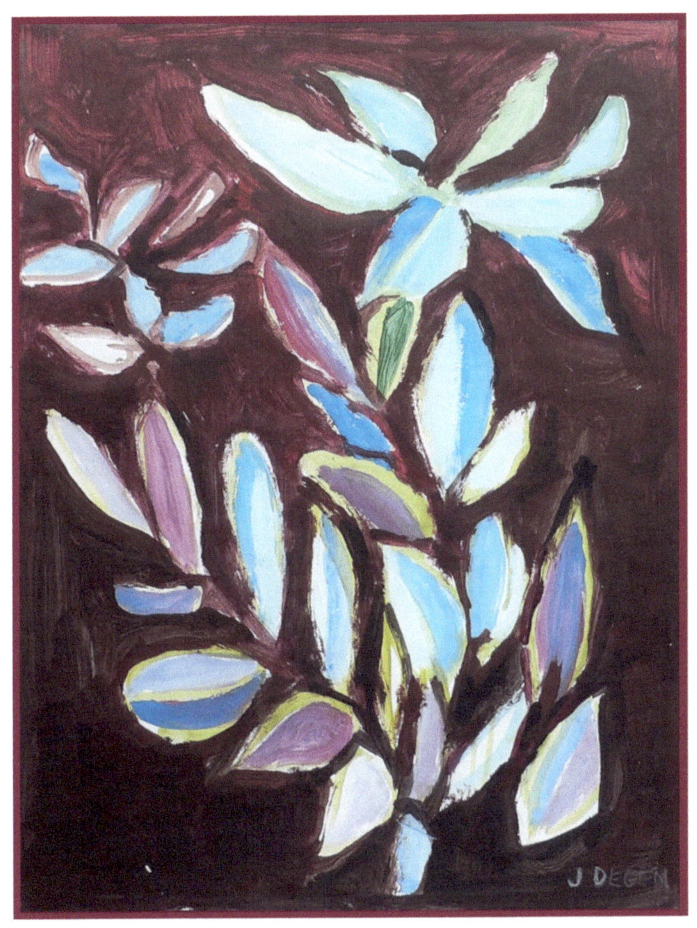

Blue Leaves

Gouache on paper, 32 x 24 cm, 2004

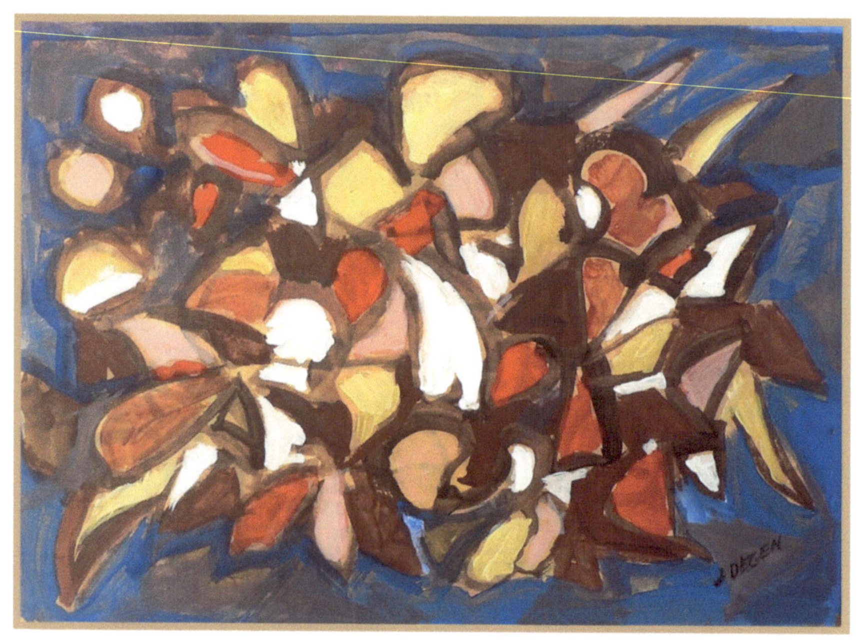

Garden Corner

Acrylic on paper, 25 x 35 cm, 2008

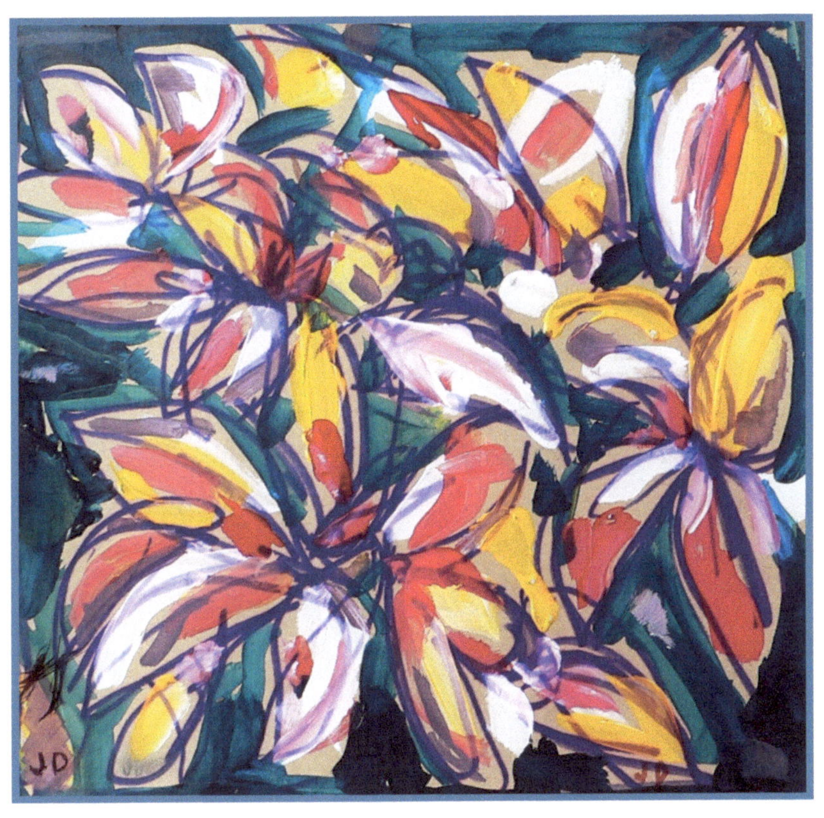

Colour in the Garden

Mixed media on paper, 27 x 27 cm, 2008

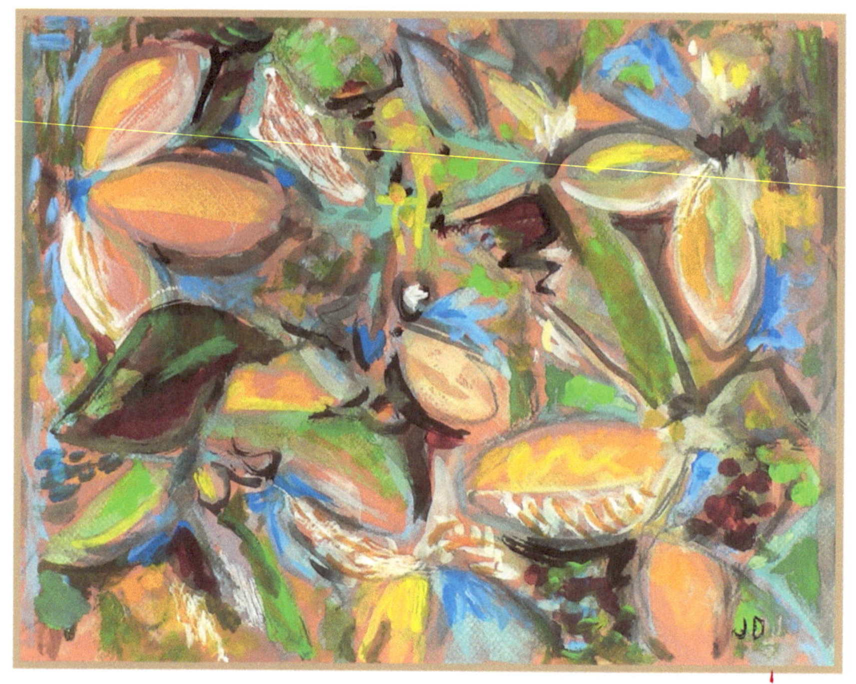

Coloured Leaves

Acrylic on paper, 28 x 36 cm, 2012

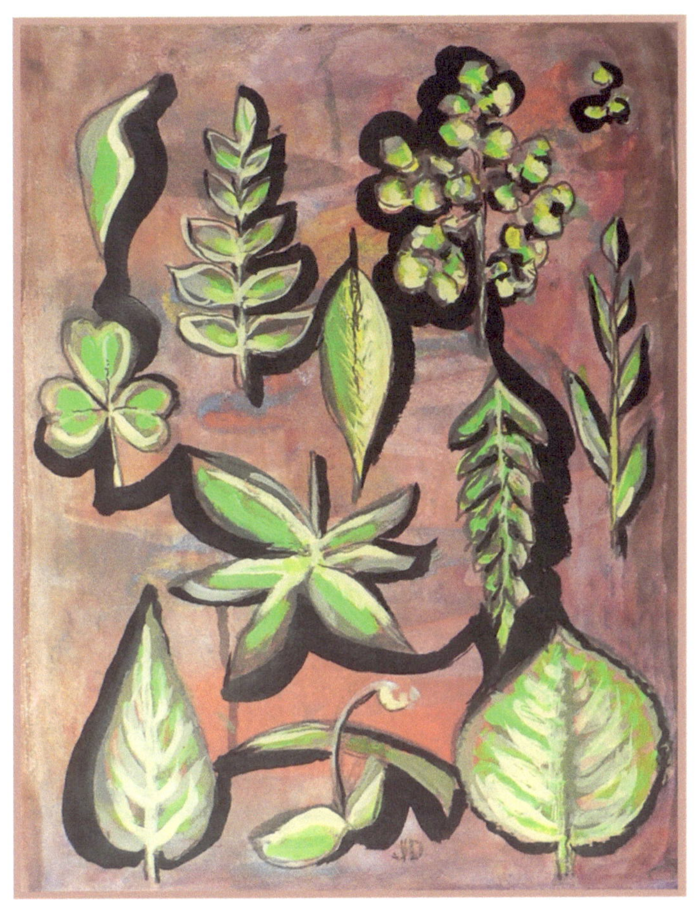

Leaves' Survey

Acrylic on paper, 38 x 29 cm, 2007

Flowers, more fleeting, more ethereal,
and more delicate than the plants
out of which they emerged,
would become like messengers from another
realm, like a bridge between the world of
physical forms and the formless.
They not only had a scent
that was delicate and pleasing to humans, but
also brought a fragrance from the realm of spirit.
(Eckhart Tolle)

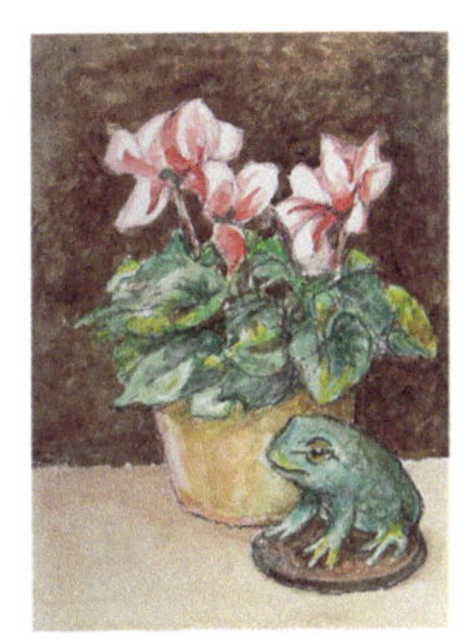

Flowering

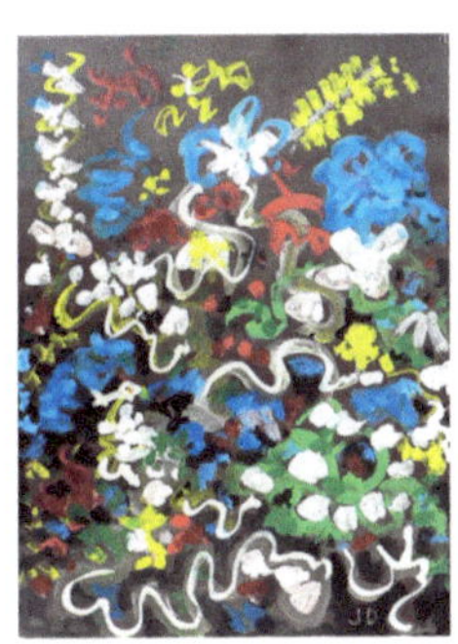

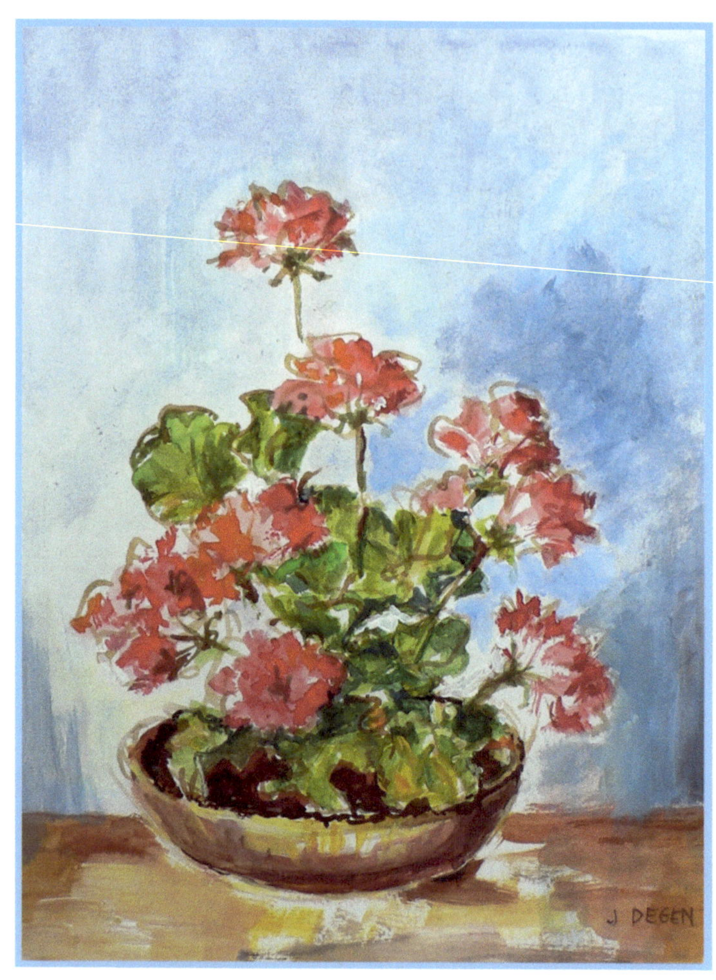

Pelargonium

Acrylic on paper, 35 x 26 cm, 2007

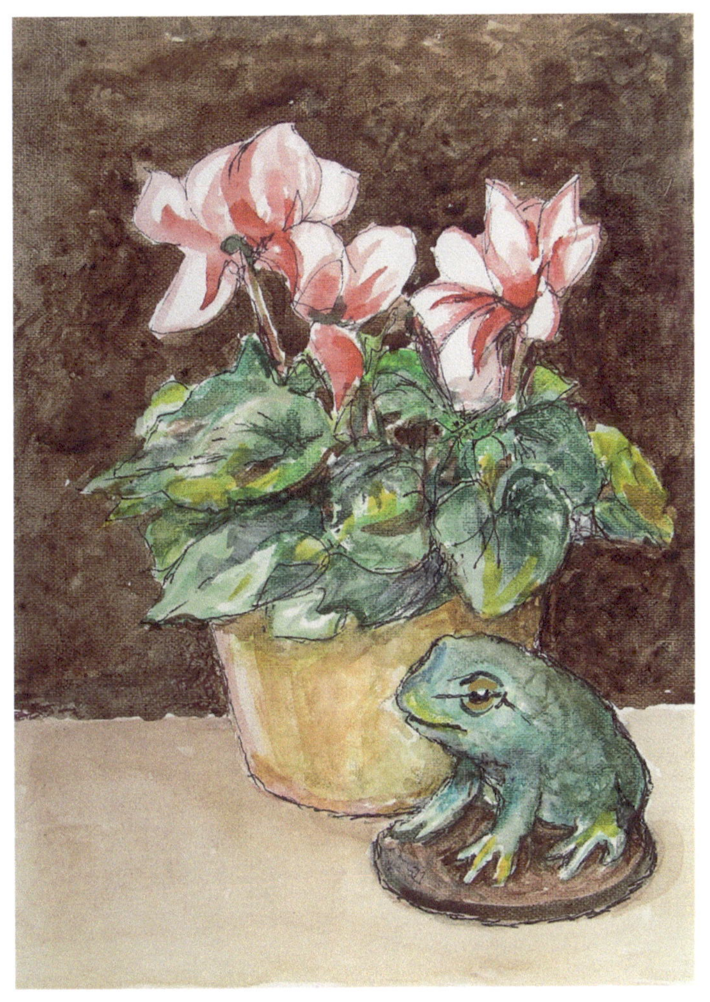

A Watch

Acrylic and pen on paper, 29 x 20 cm, 2008

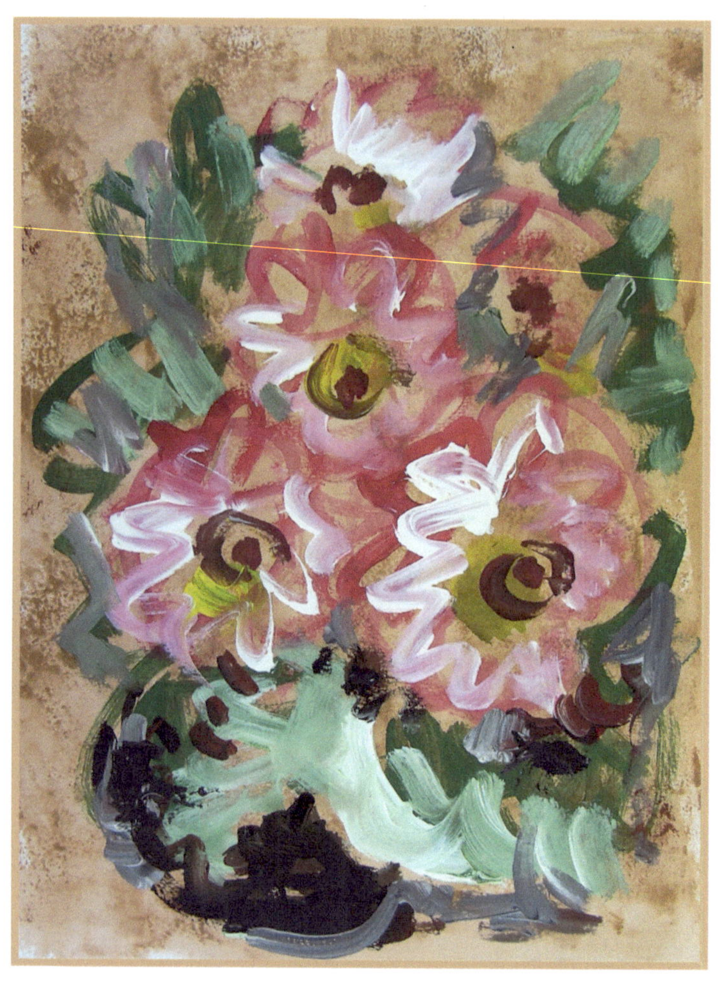

Flowering

Acrylic on paper, 37 x 28 cm, 2009

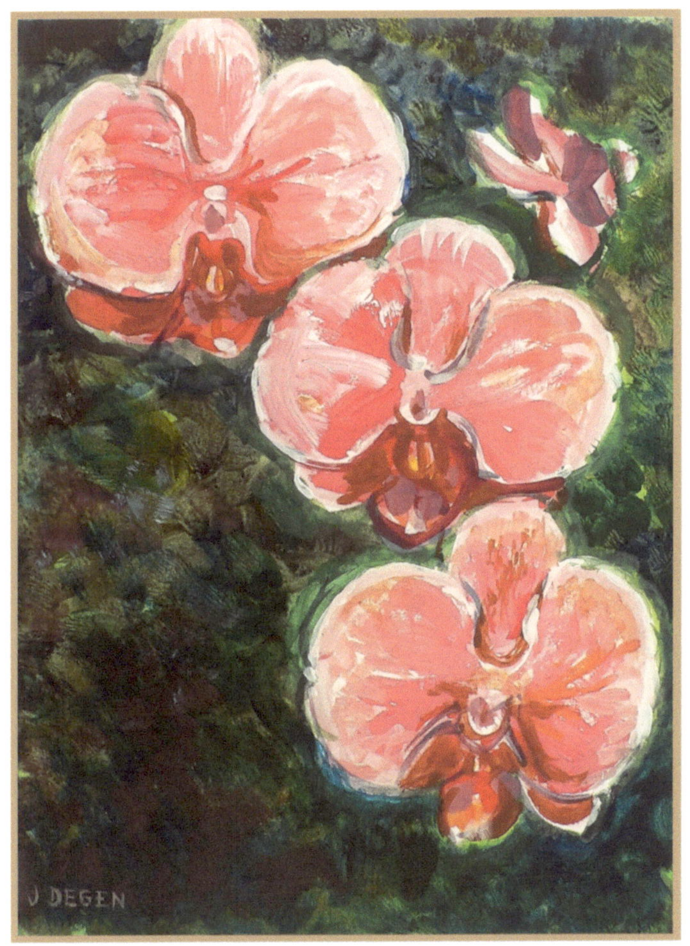

Three Sisters

Acrylic on paper, 36 x 26 cm, 2007

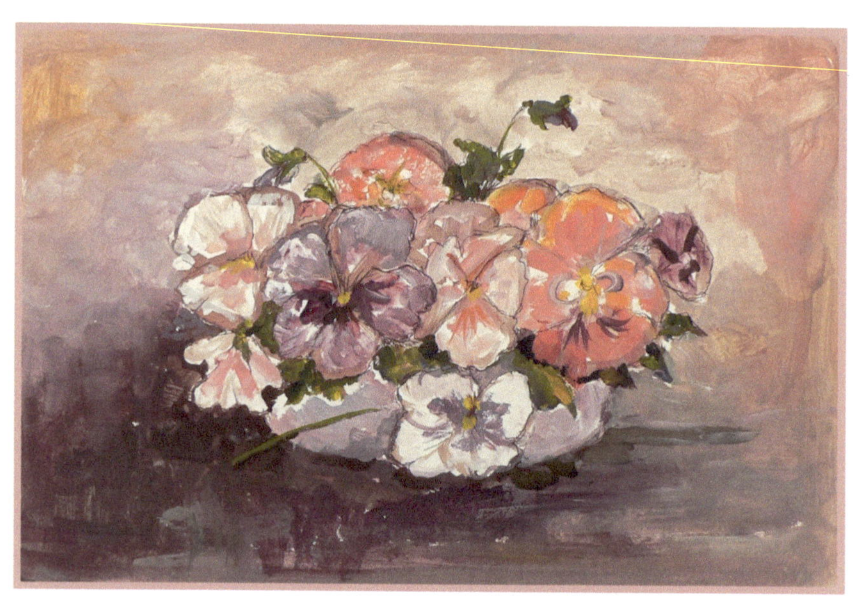

Pansies

Acrylic on paper, 23 x 34 cm, 2002

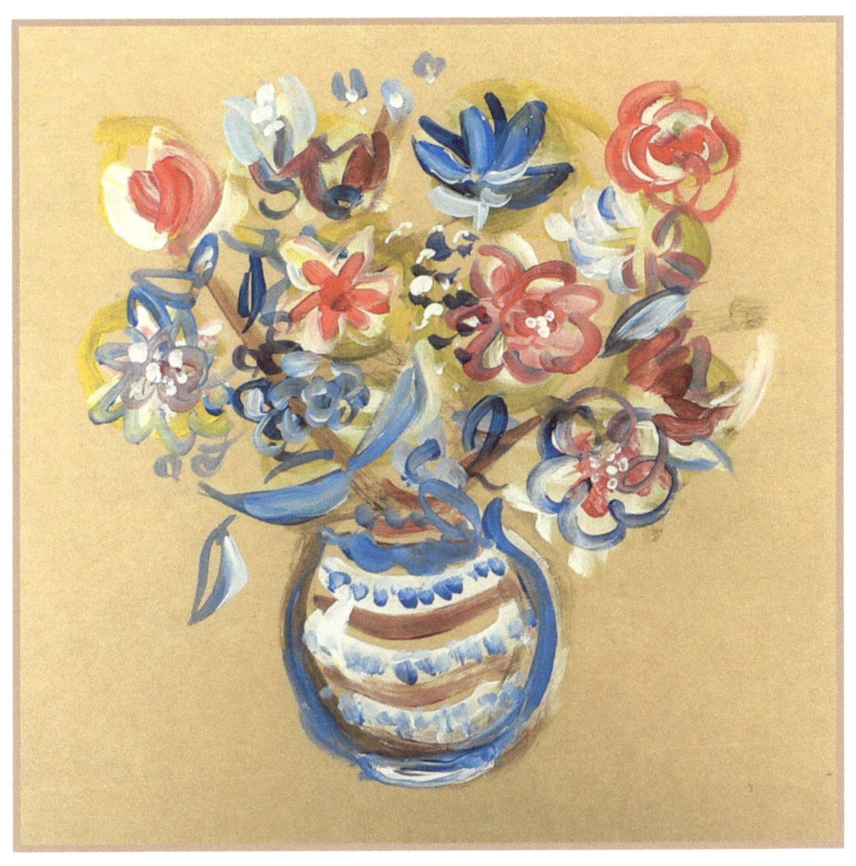

A Simple Bouquet

Acrylic on paper, 27 x 27 cm, 2003

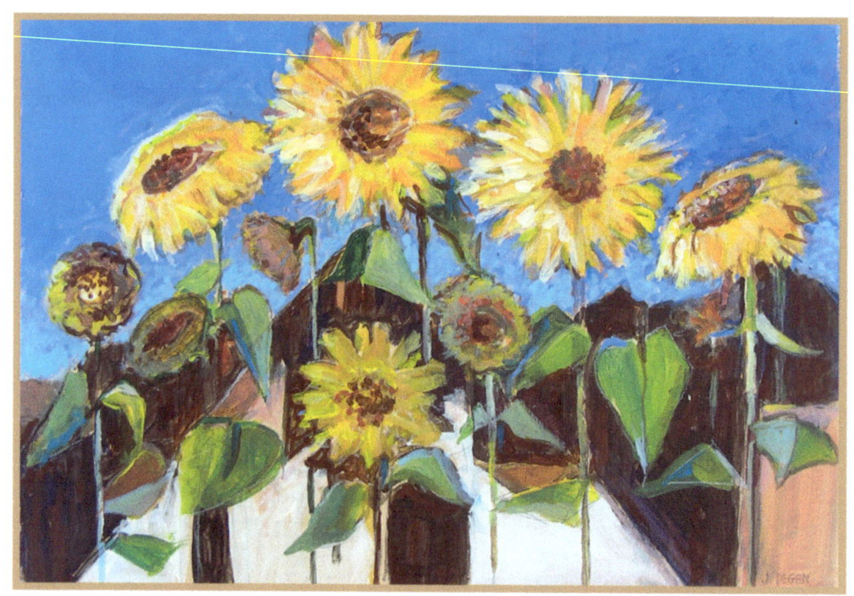

Sunflowers

Acrylic on paper, 20 x 28 cm, 2013

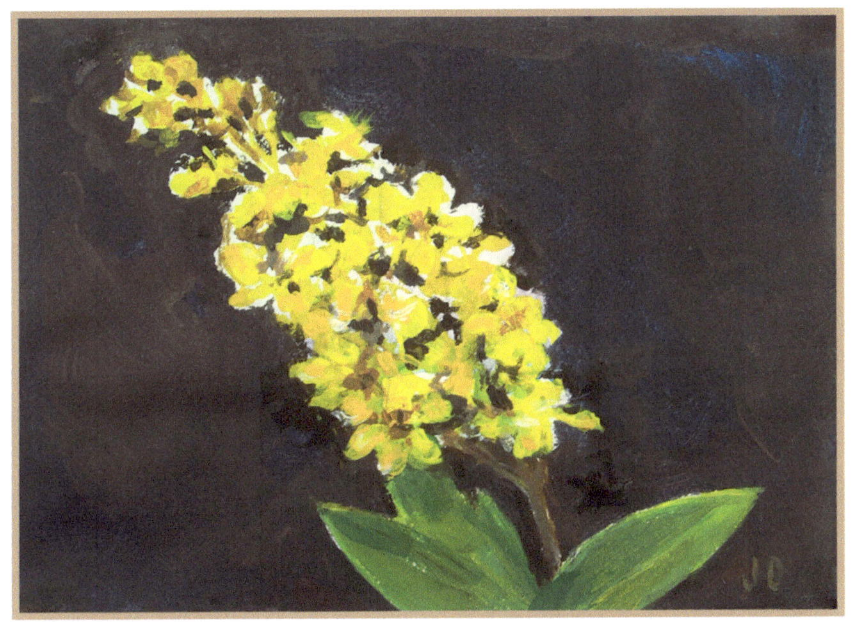

Modesty

Acrylic on paper, 20 x 26 cm, 2009

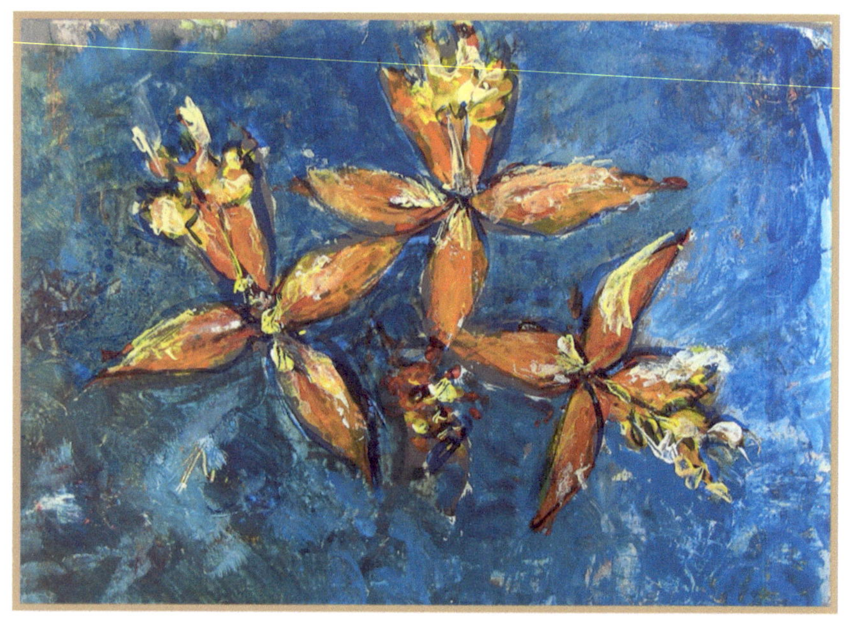

Orange Flowers

Oil on paper, 27 x 38 cm, 2005

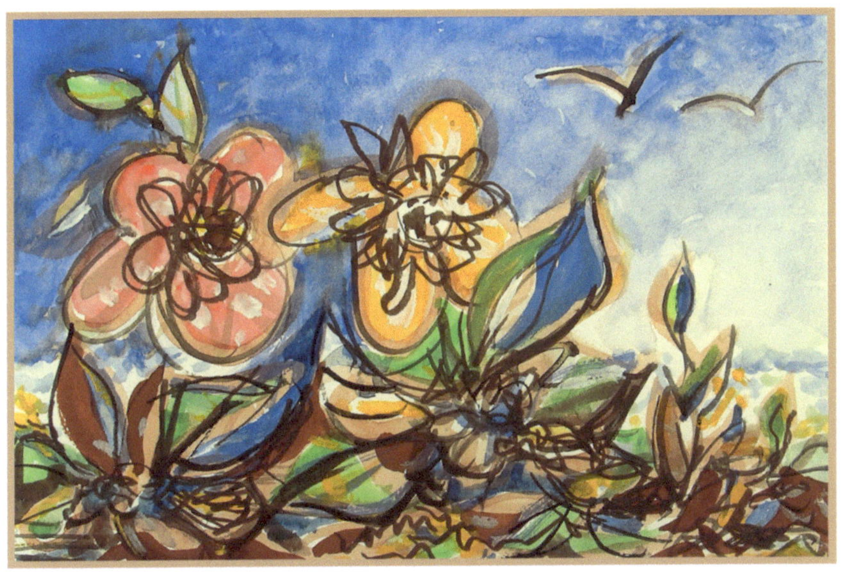

Birds Overhead

Mixed media on paper, 21 x 26 cm, 2010

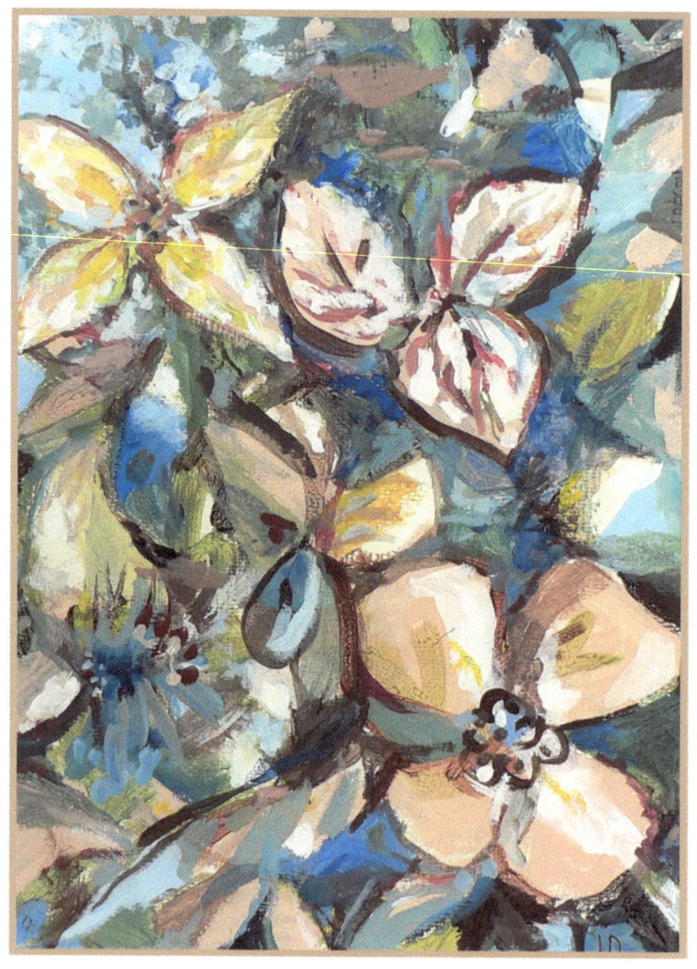

Luxuriance

Acrylic on paper, 38 x 28 cm, 2006

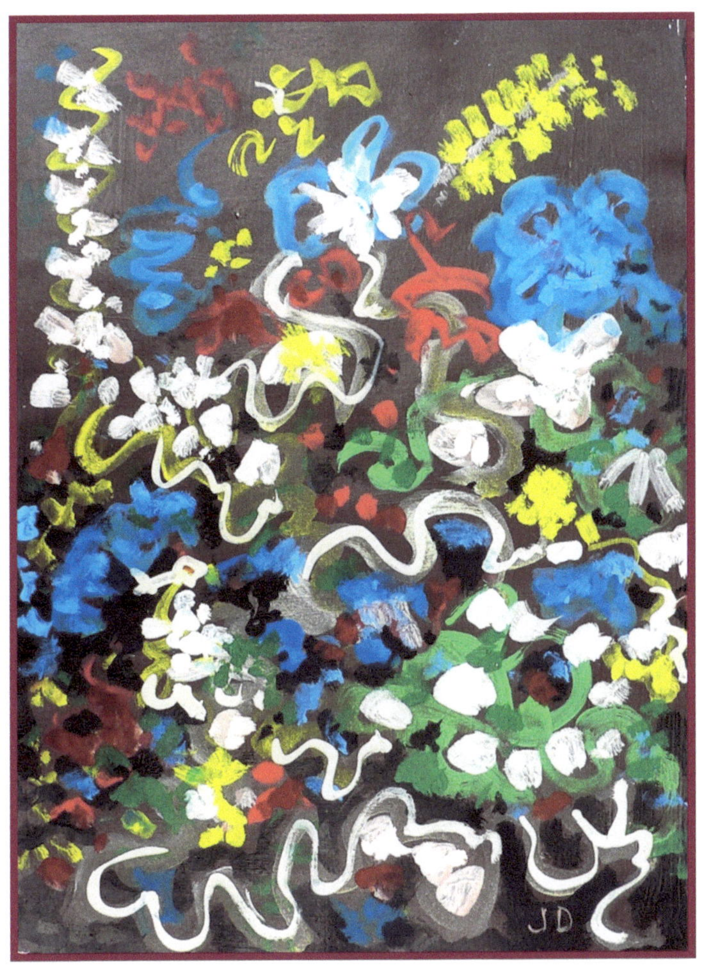

Blossoms

Acrylic on paper, 37 x 27 cm, 2012

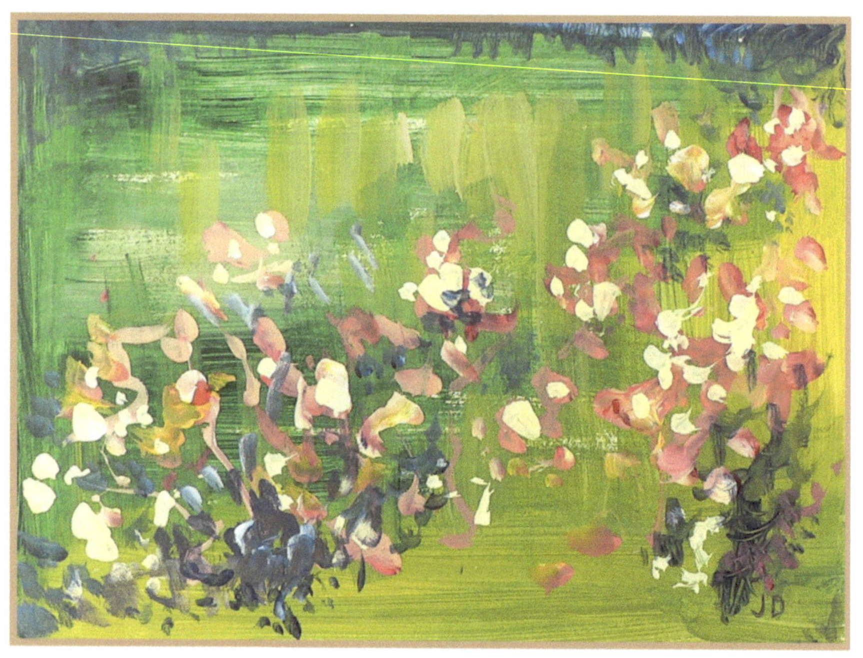

Flower Beds

Acrylic on paper, 23 x 31 cm, 1993

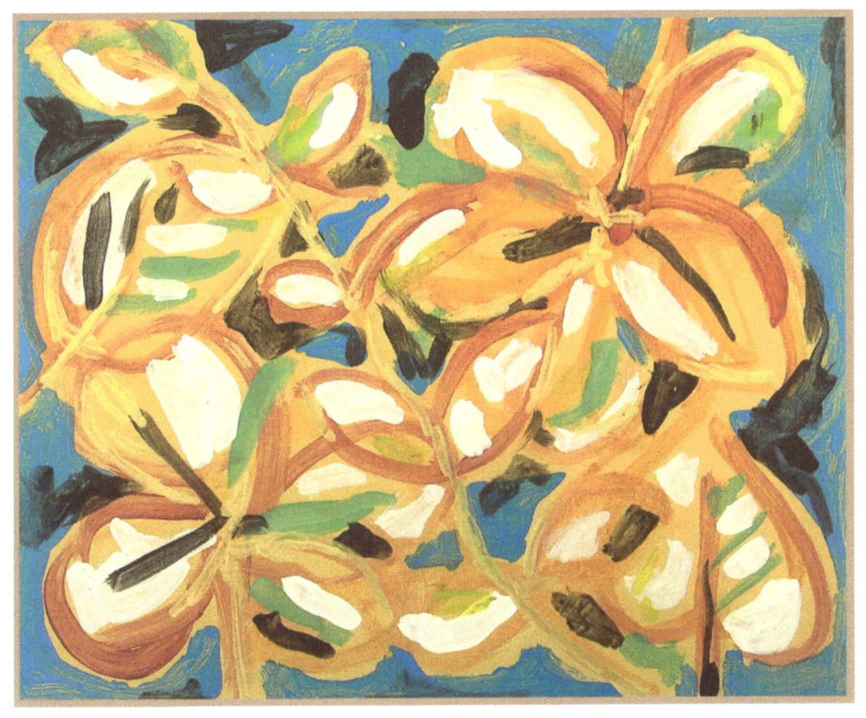

Golden Leaves

Mixed media on board, 21 x 25 cm, 2013

Animals are such agreeable friends -
they ask no questions, they pass no criticisms.
(George Eliot)

In order to keep a true perspective
of one's importance,
everyone should have a dog that will worship him
and a cat that will ignore him.
(Dereke Bruce)

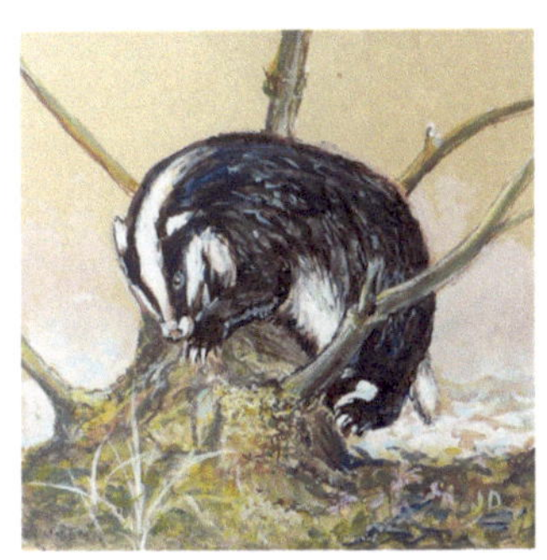

Living Creatures

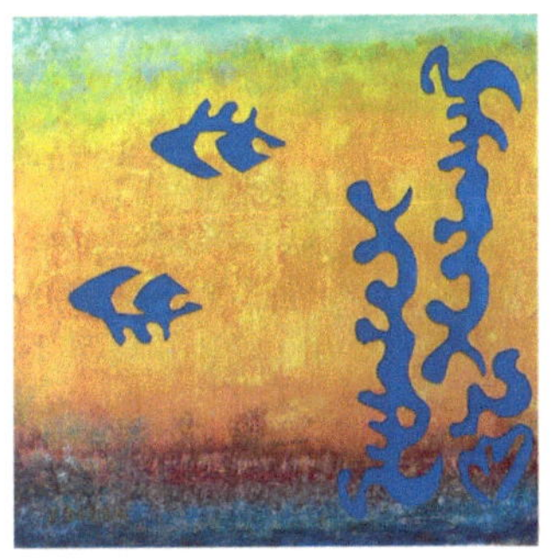

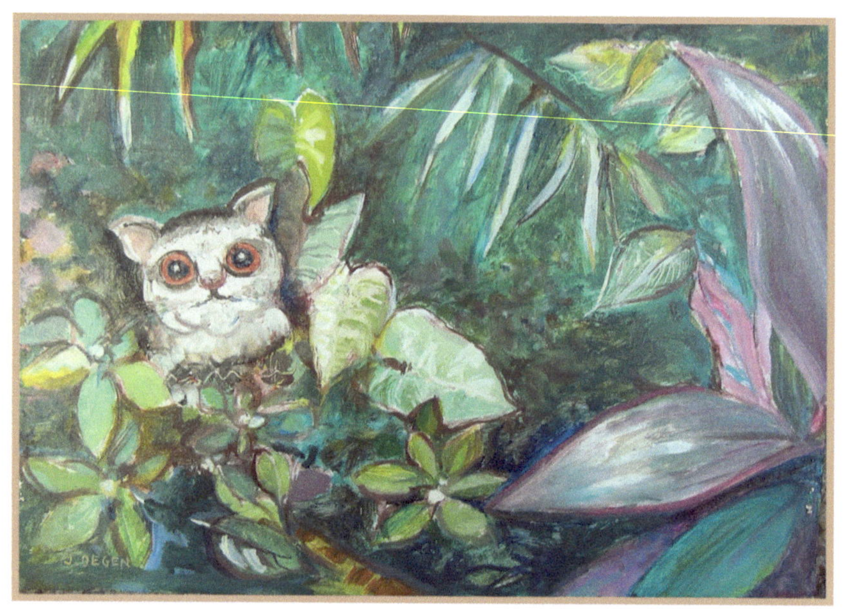

Cat Scarecrow

Oil on board, 27 x 38 cm, 2002

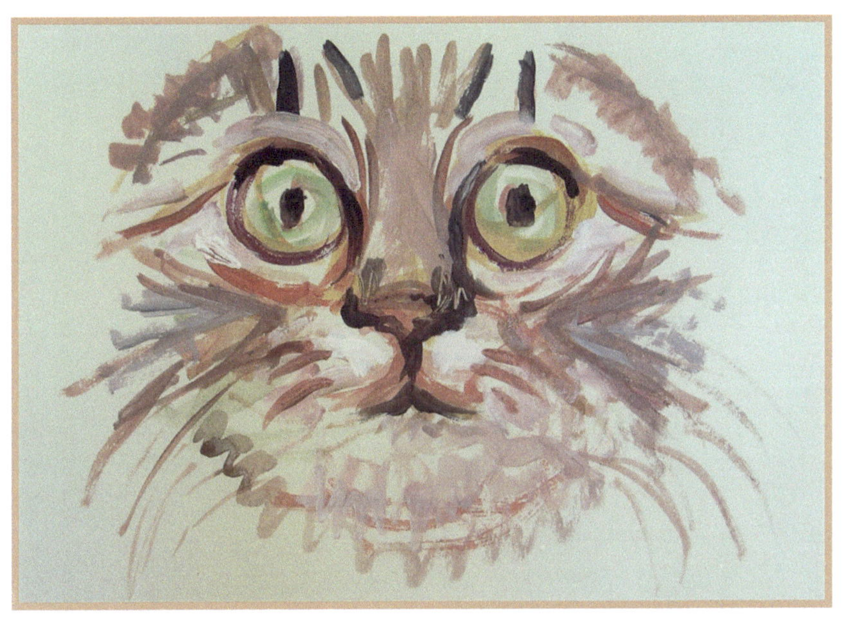

Big Cat

Acrylic on paper, 28 x 37 cm, 2004

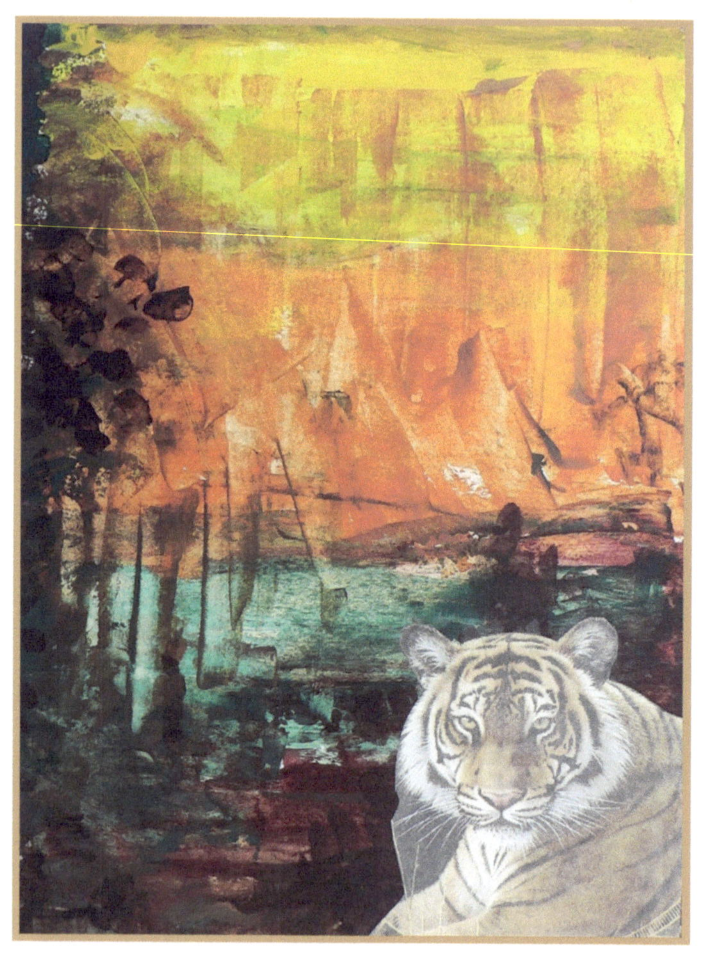

Undisturbed

Collage on paper, 30 x 22 cm, 2002

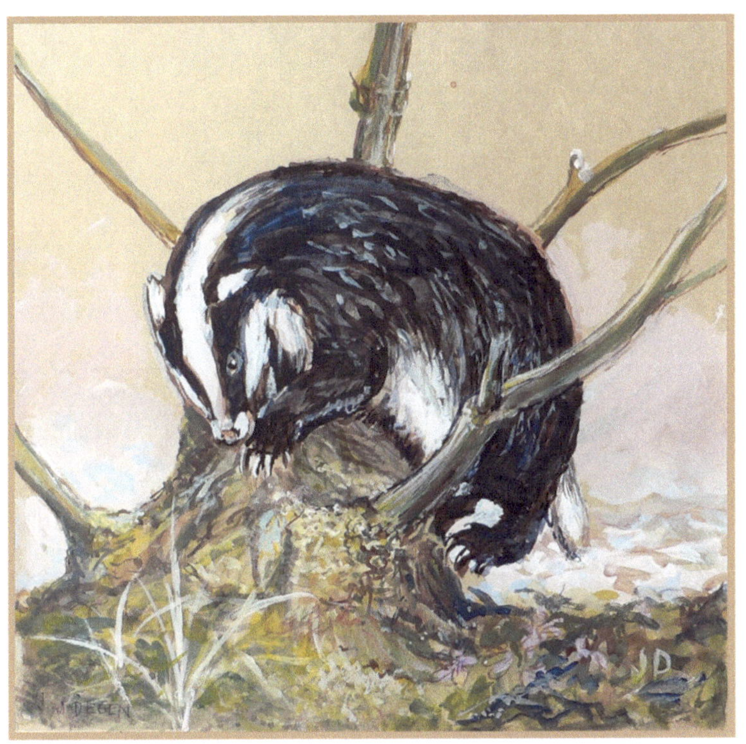

Badger

Acrylic on paper, 28 x 28 cm, 2003

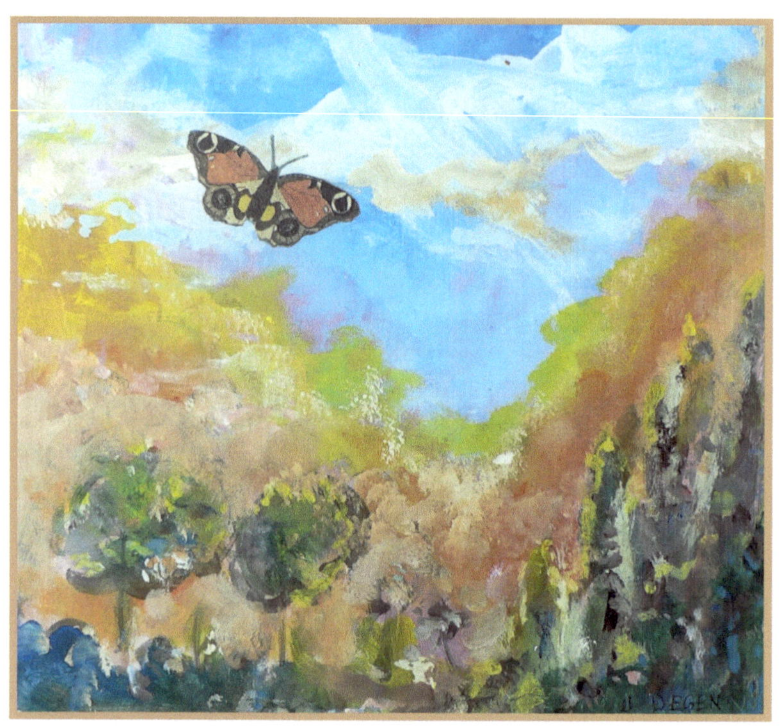

Butterfly

Mixed media on paper, 28 x 28 cm, 2006

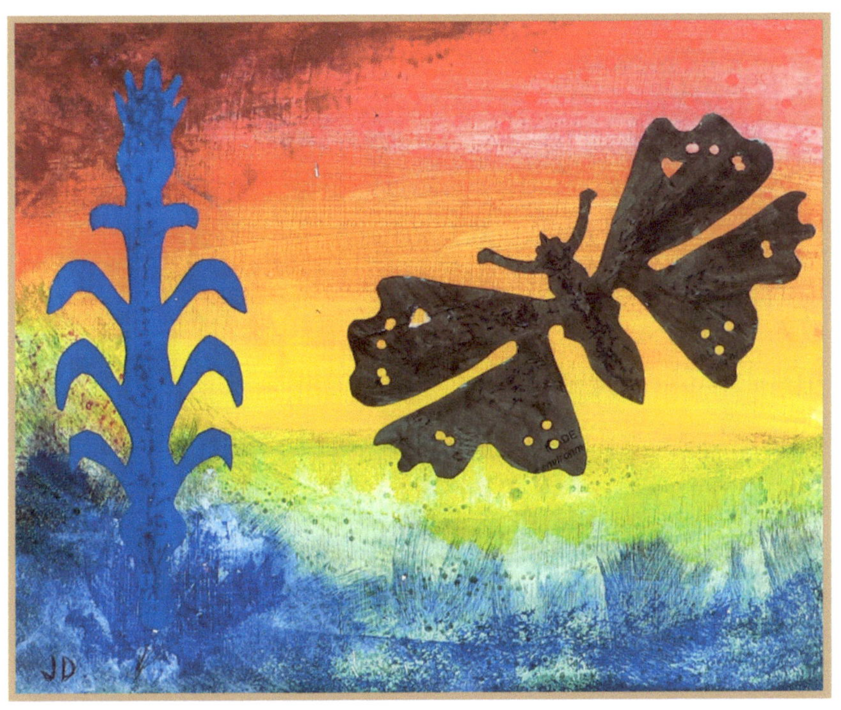

Night Coming

Collage on paper, 25 x 28 cm, 2000

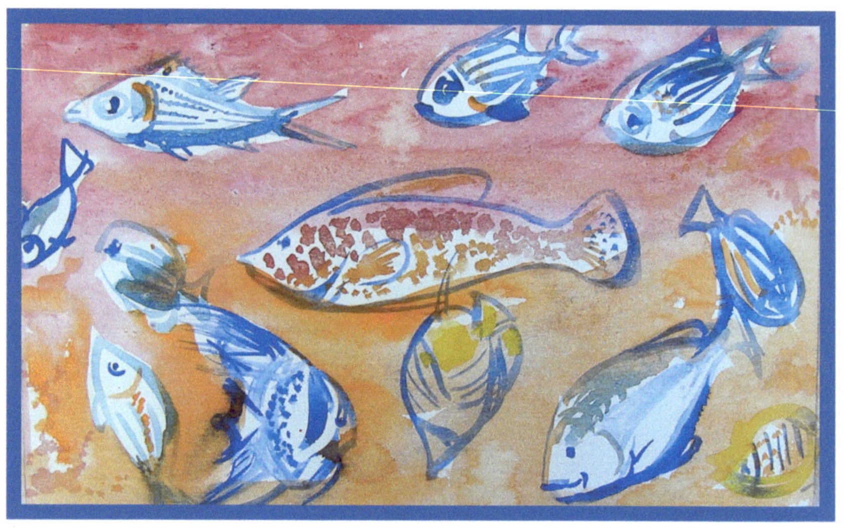

Fish

Watercolour on paper, 23 x 37 cm, 2003

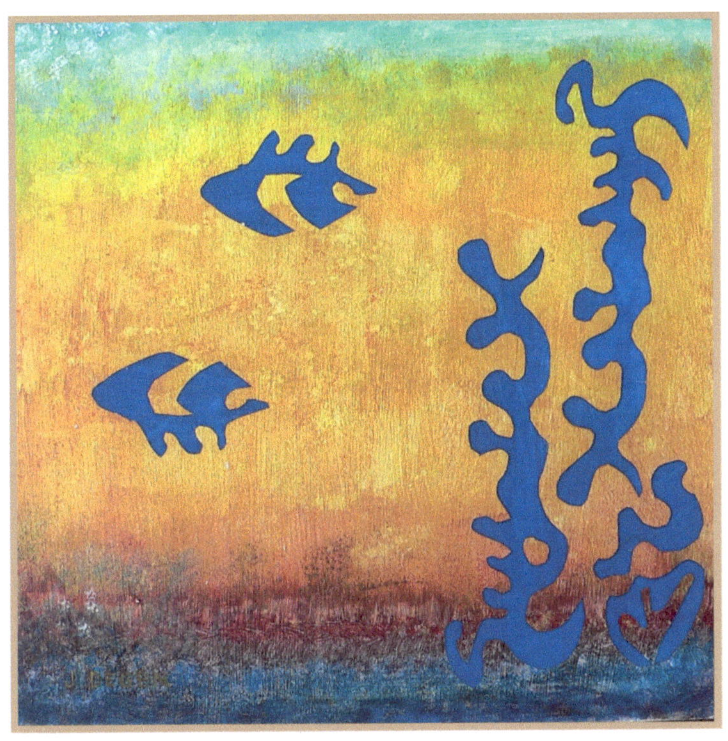

Deep Sea

Mixed media on paper, 24 x 24 cm, 2006

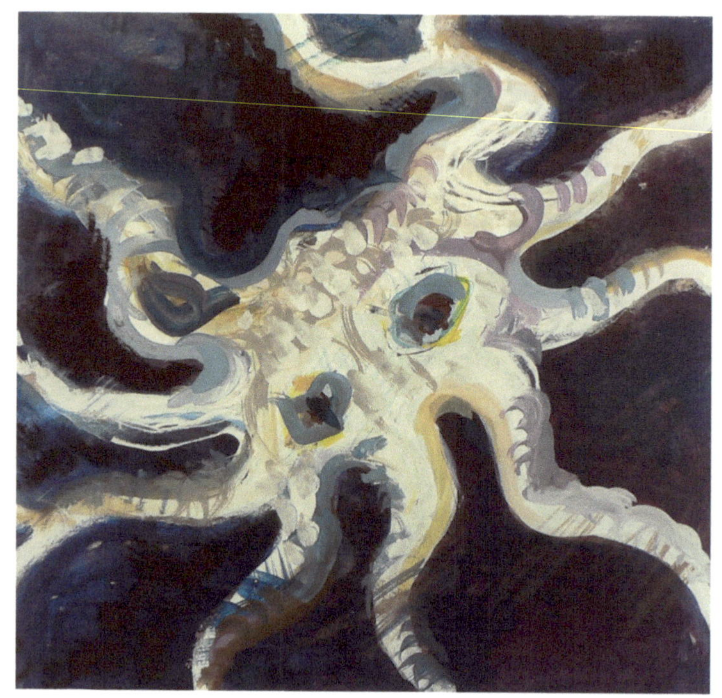

Octopus

Acrylic on paper, 29 x 29 cm, 2006

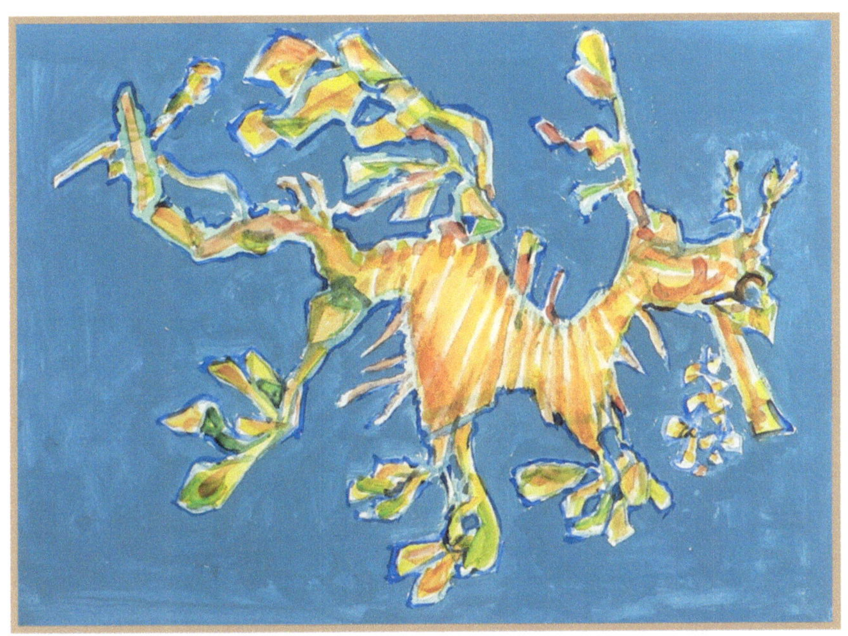

Seahorse

Acrylic on paper, 27 x 37 cm, 2003

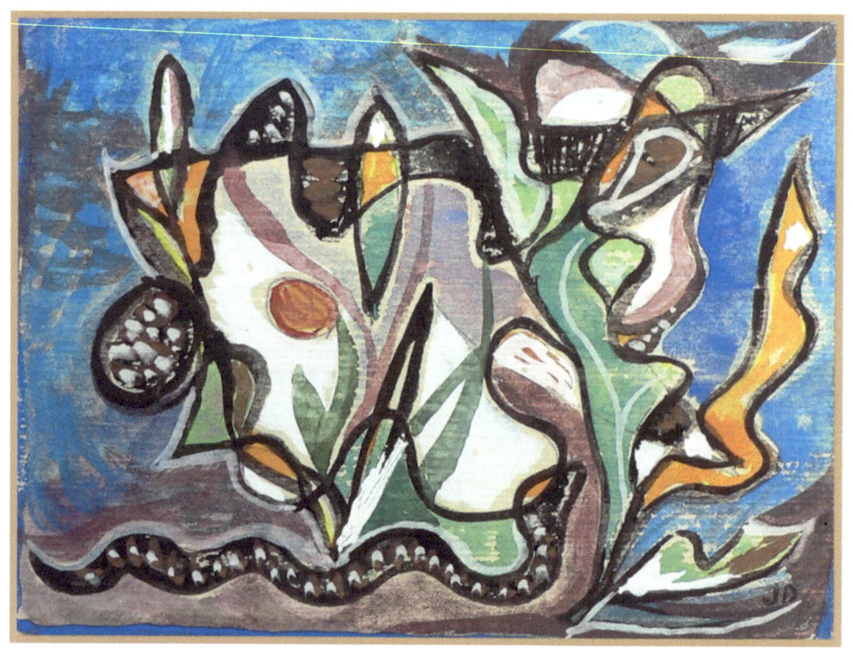

Snakes Visiting

Gouache on paper, 22 x 29 cm, 2007

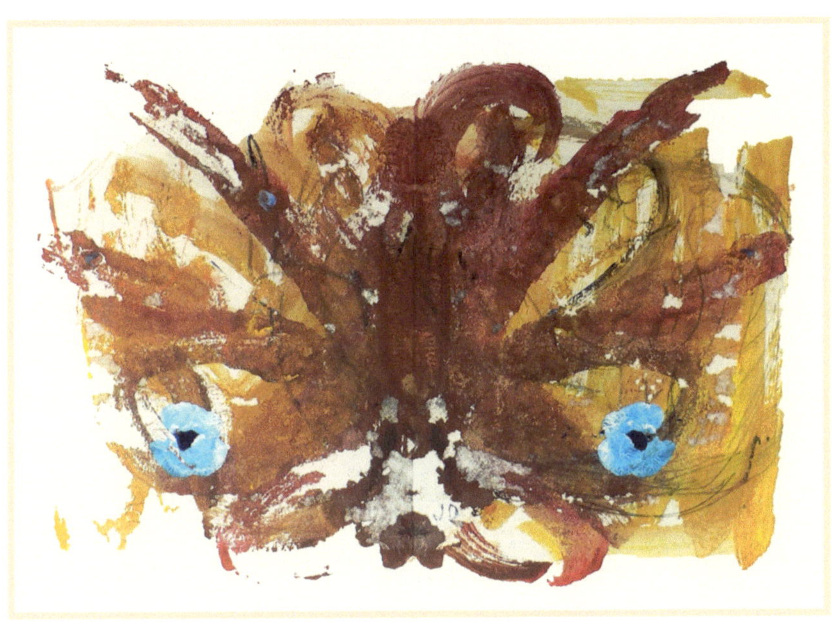

Lurking

Monoprint on paper, 28 x 37 cm, 2006

The painter thinks in forms and colours.
The object is poetry.
(George Braque)

Art does not reproduce the visible;
rather, it makes visible.
(Paul Klee)

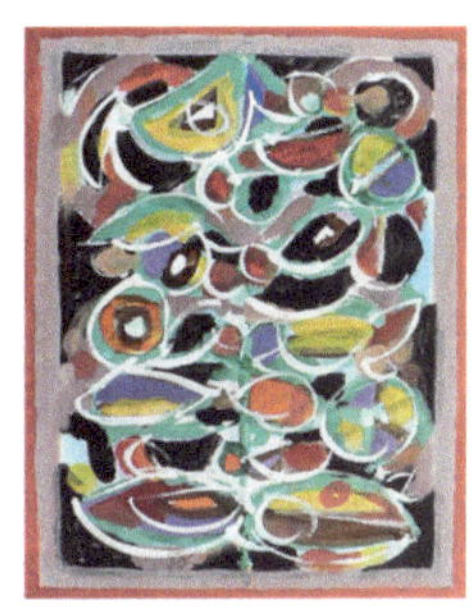

Spatial

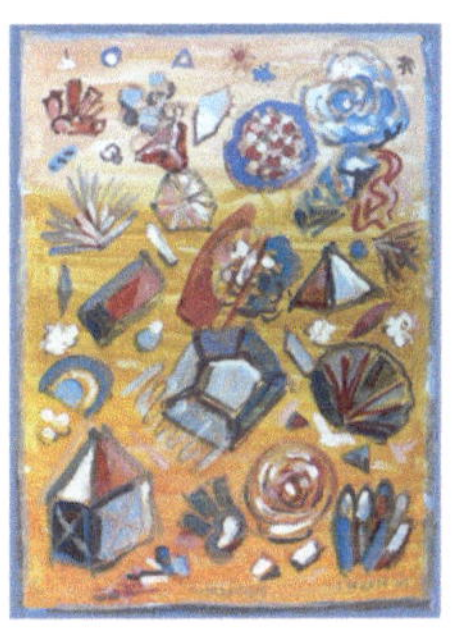

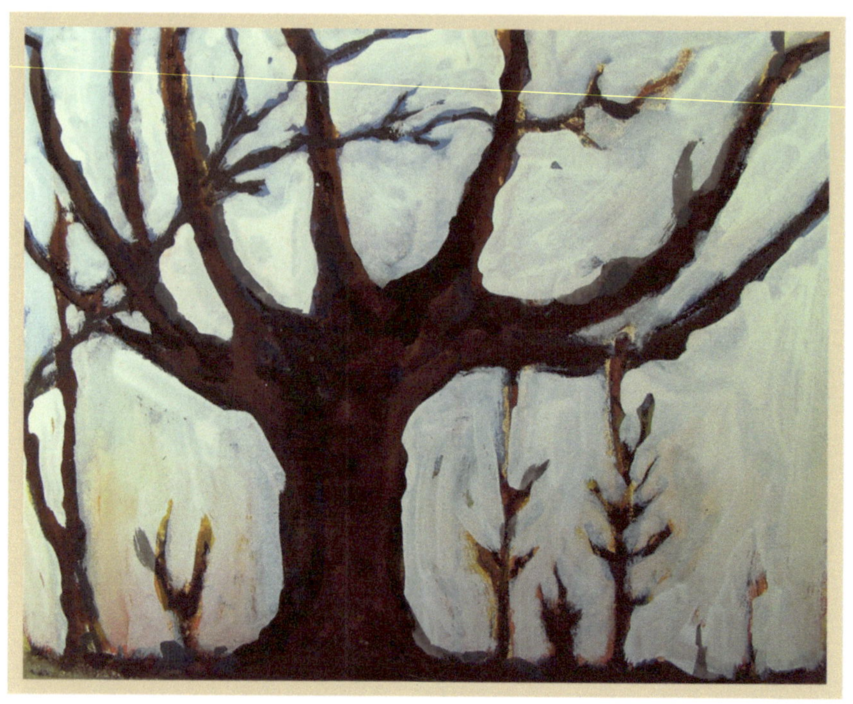

Tree

Acrylic on canvas, 40 x 49 cm, 1988

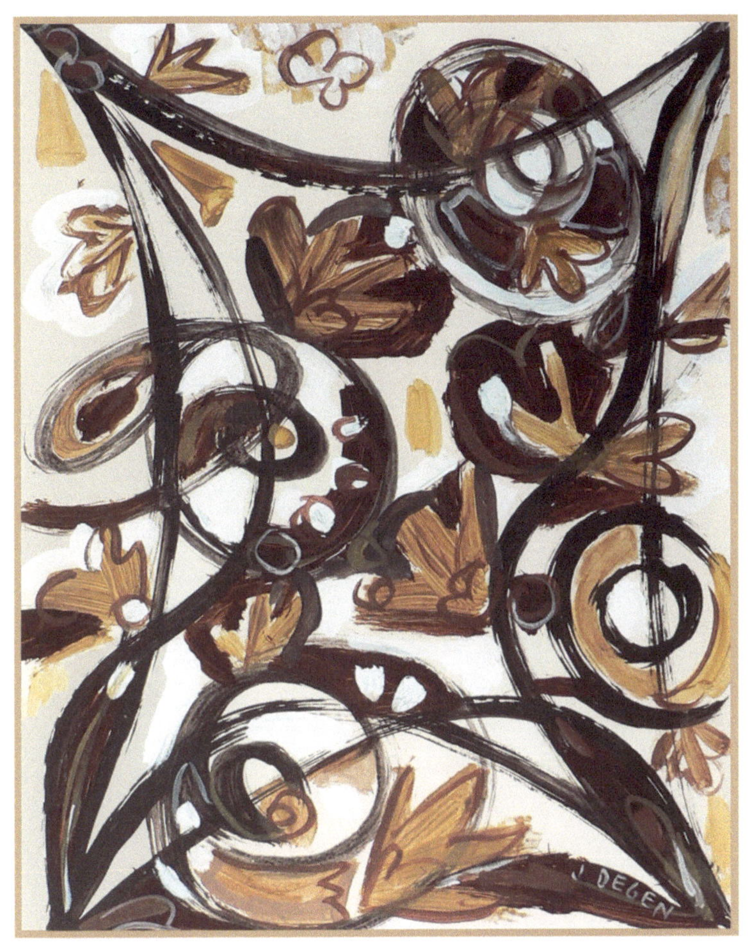

Garden View

Acrylic on paper board, 33 x 25 cm, 2004

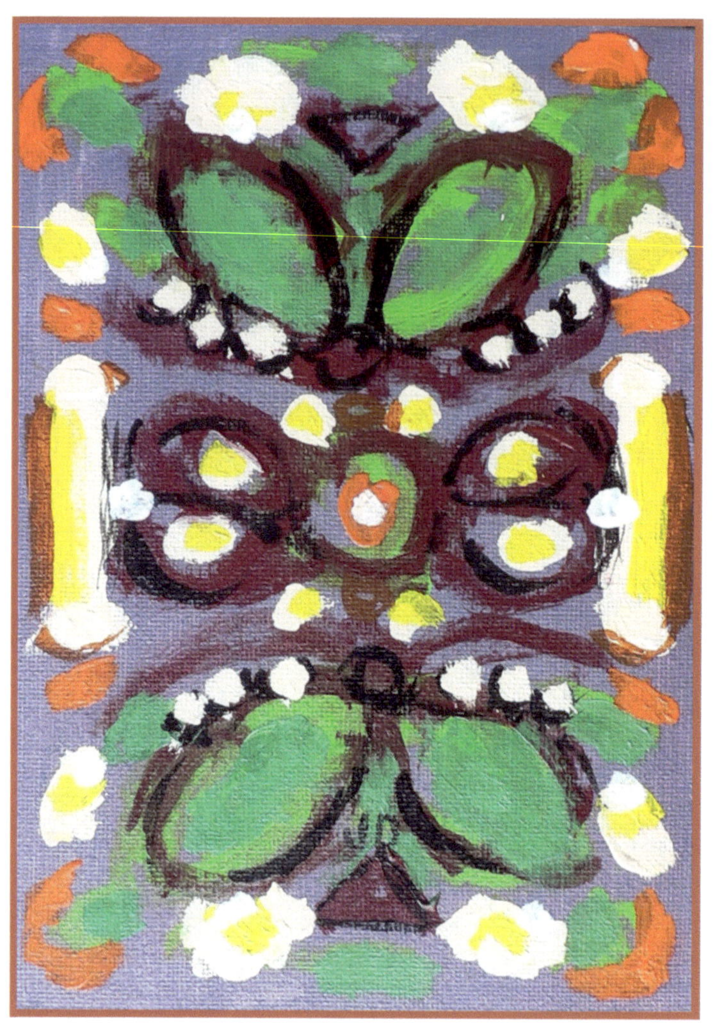

Mirroring

Acrylic on board, 22 x 16 cm, 2012

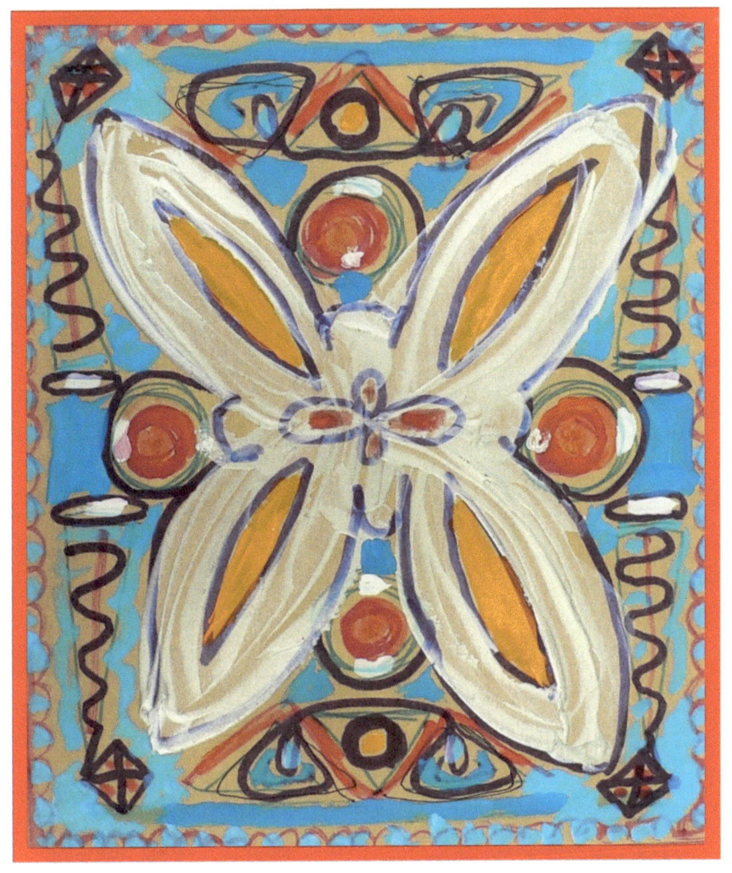

Silver Flower

Mixed media on paper, 27 x 22 cm 2005

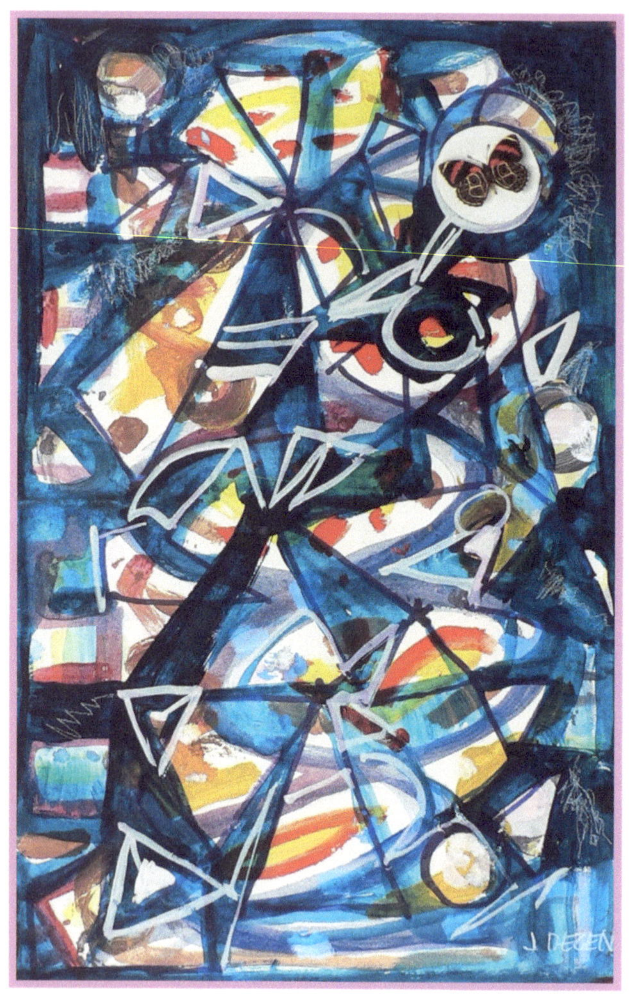

Butterfly Investigation

Mixed media on paper, 39 x 25 cm, 2004

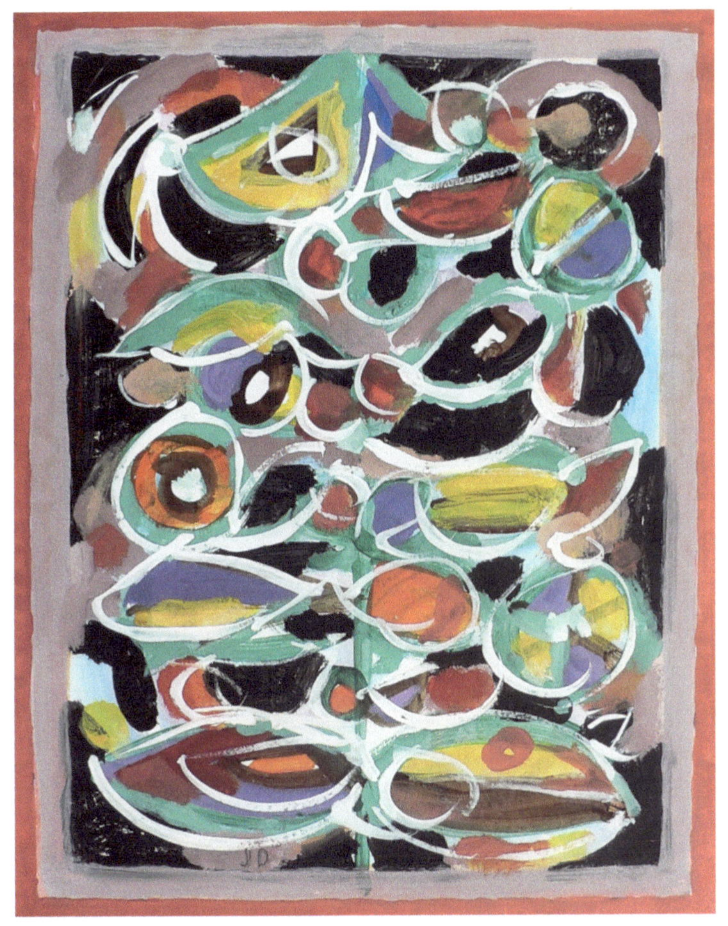

Fruity Picking

Acrylic on paper, 35 x 27 cm, 2004

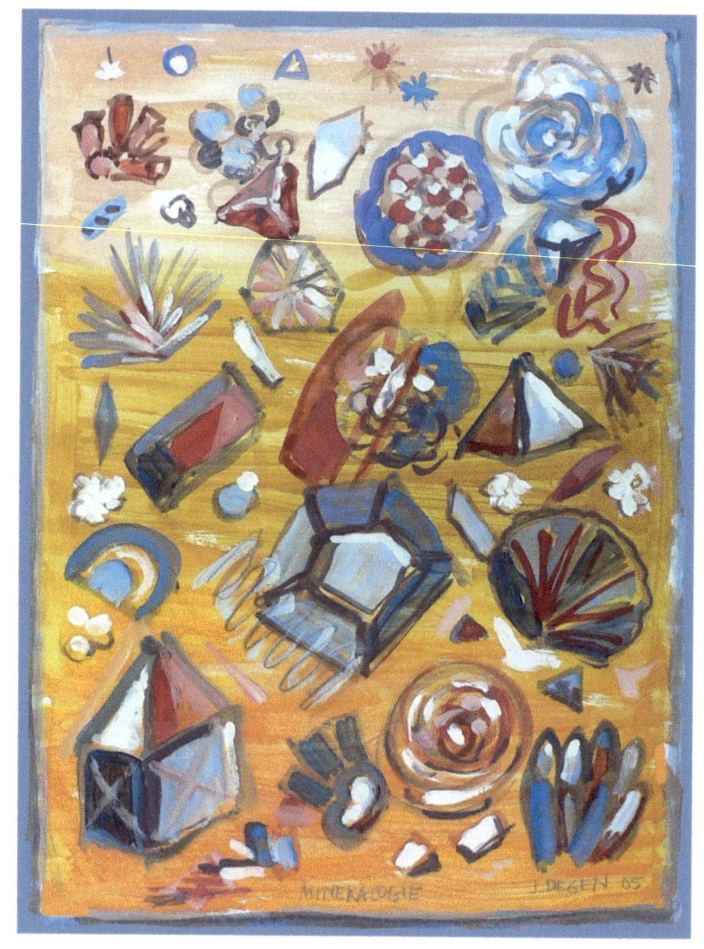

Mineralogy

Acrylic on paper, 40 x 29 cm, 2005

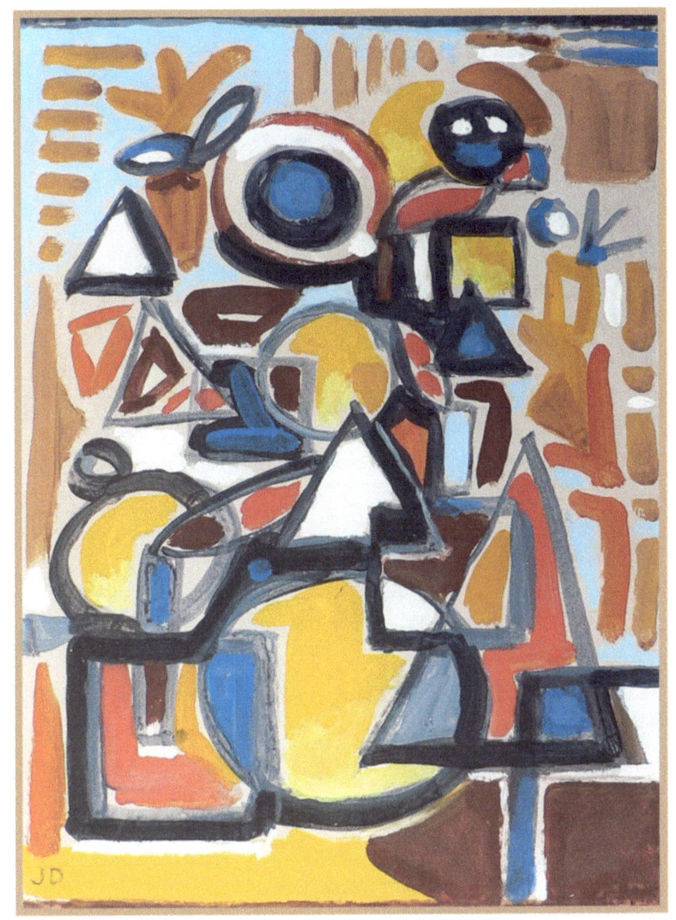

Yellow Road

Gouache on board, 41 x 29 cm, 2005

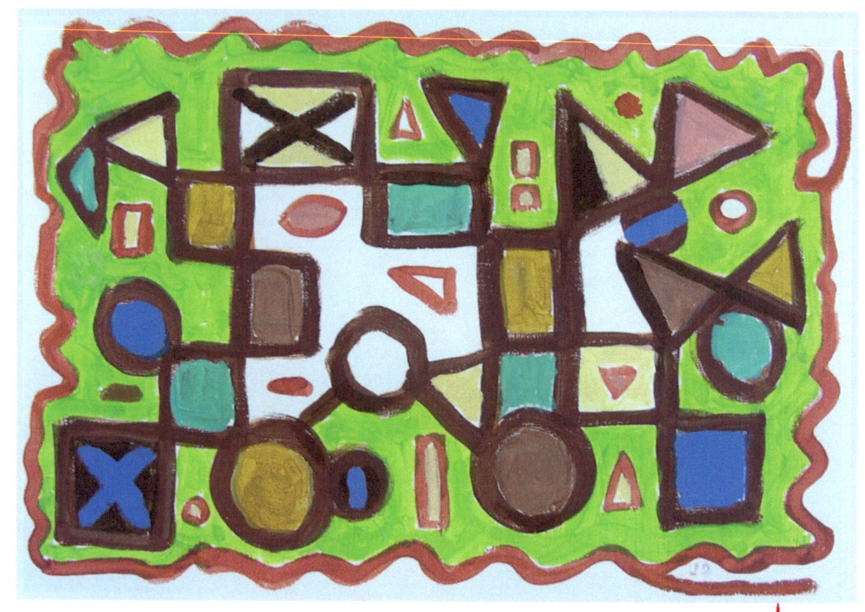

Open Garden

Acrylic on paper, 30 x 41 cm, 2009

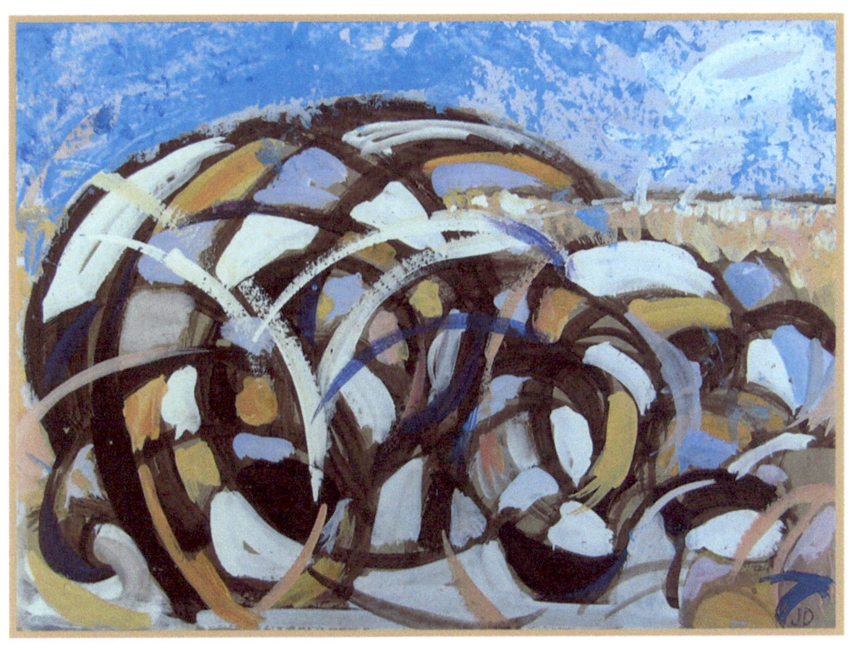

Waves Coming

Acrylic on paper, 27 x 36 cm, 2005

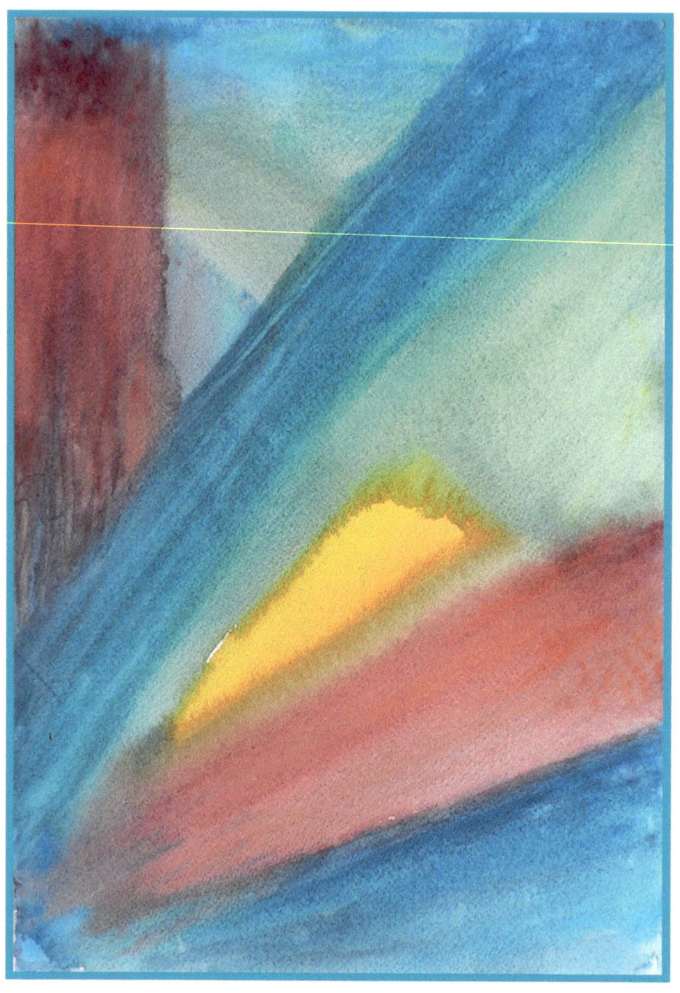

Streams

Watercolour on paper, 40 x 27 cm, 2007

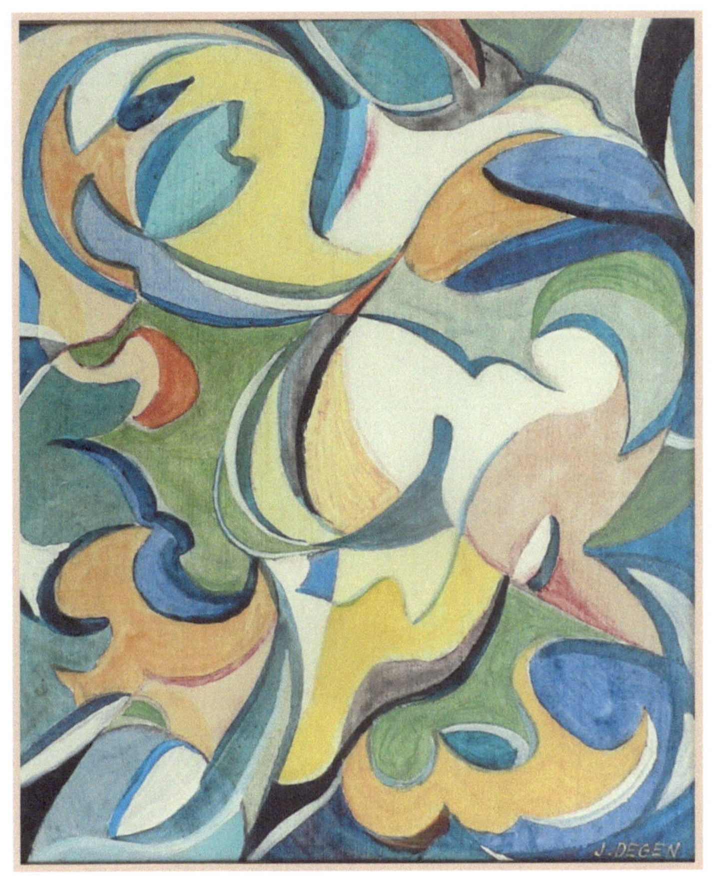

Little Garden

Gouache on board, 26 x 21 cm, 1983

*Nature is not only what is visible to the eye
– it also shows the inner images of the soul –
the images on the back side of the eyes.
(Edvard Munch)*

*Art is the unceasing effort to compete
with the beauty of flowers and never succeeding.
(Marc Chagall)*

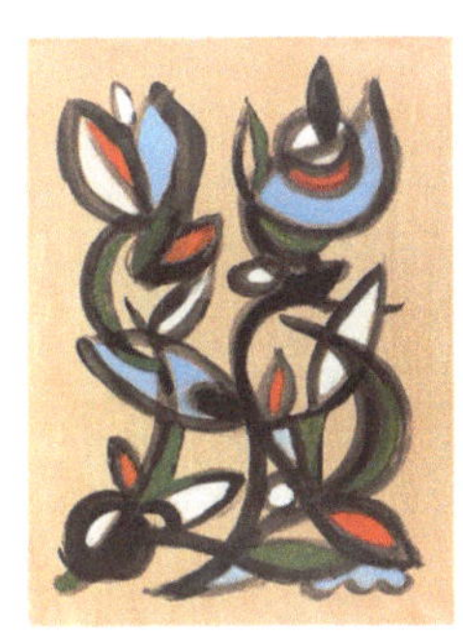

Floral Inspiration

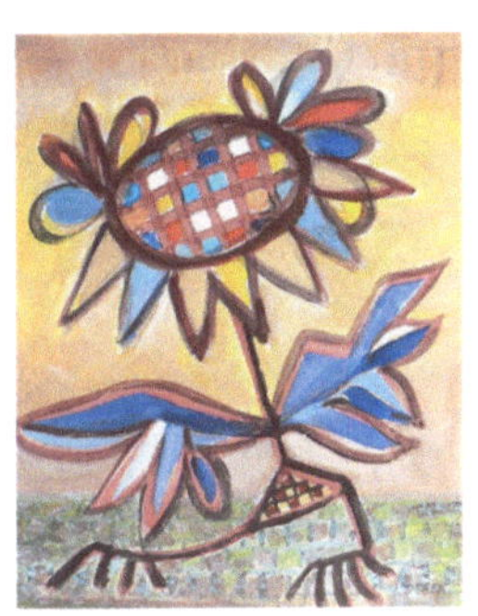

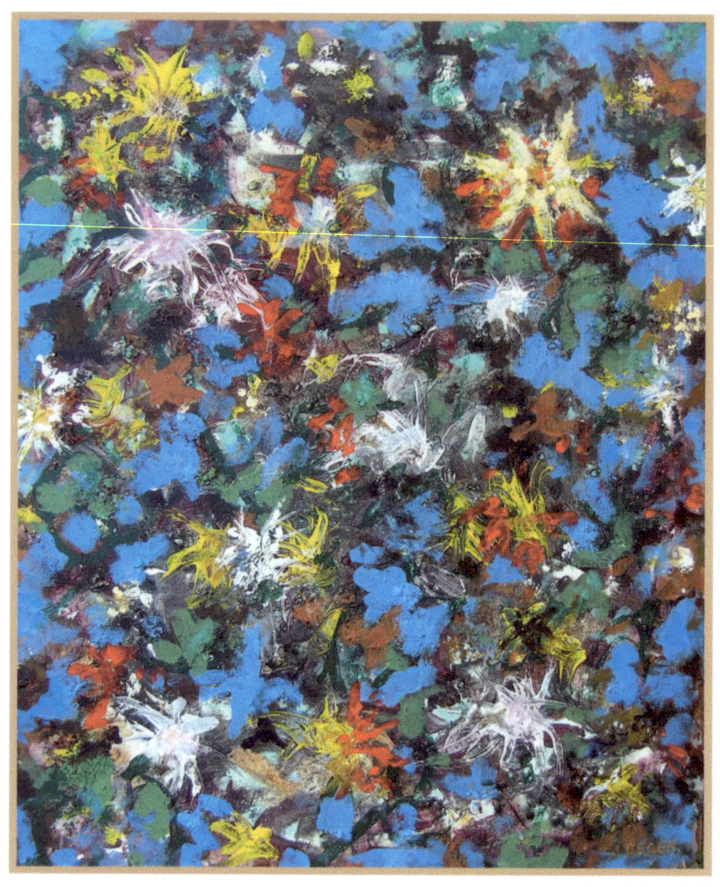

Lush Surroundings

Acrylic on board, 85 x 68 cm, 2012

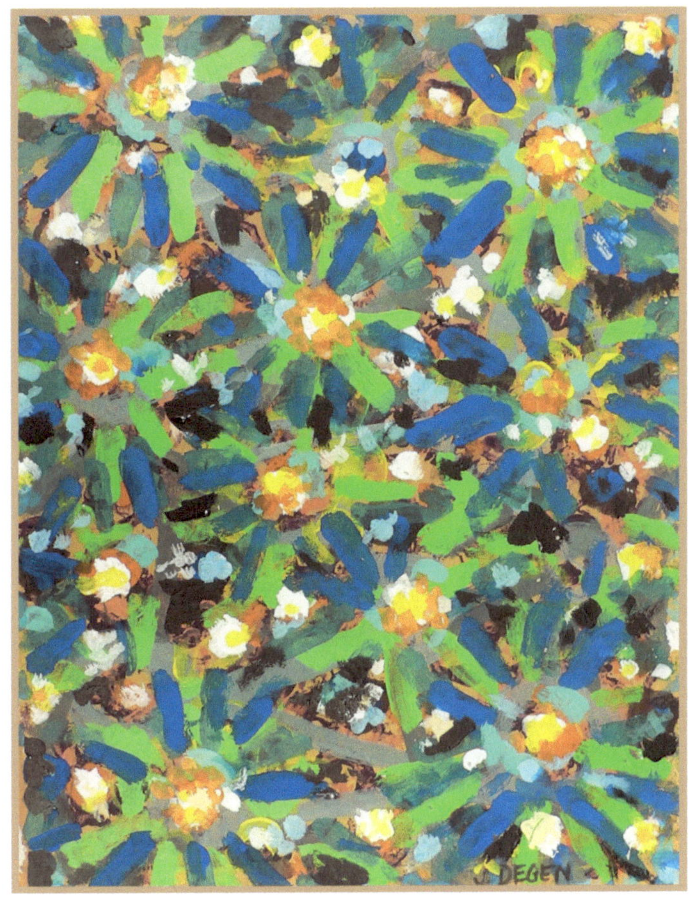

Living Pattern

Acrylic on board, 38 x 28 cm, 2010

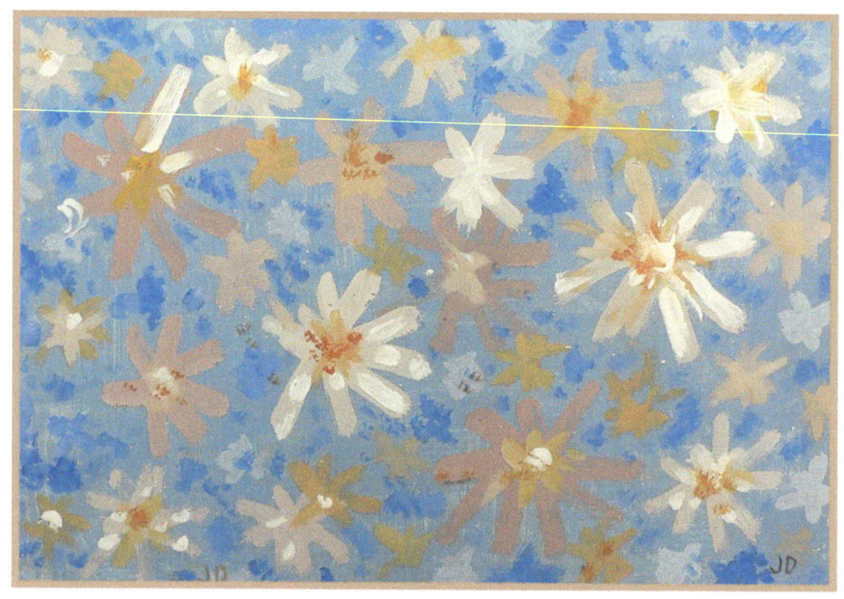

Softly Flowering

Gouache on board, 25 x 35 cm, 1985

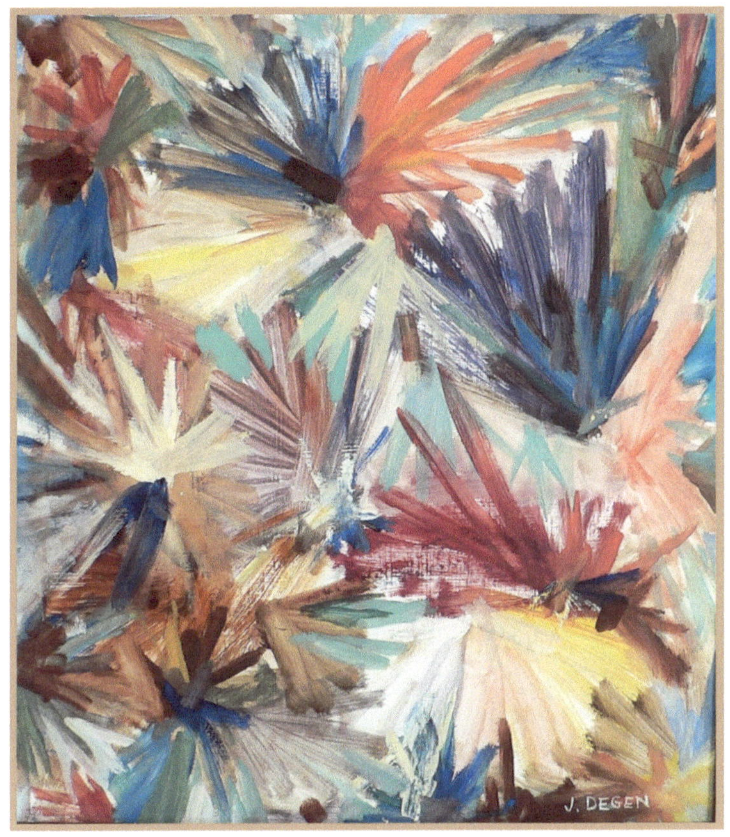

Petals

Oil on board, 52 x 45 cm, 1987

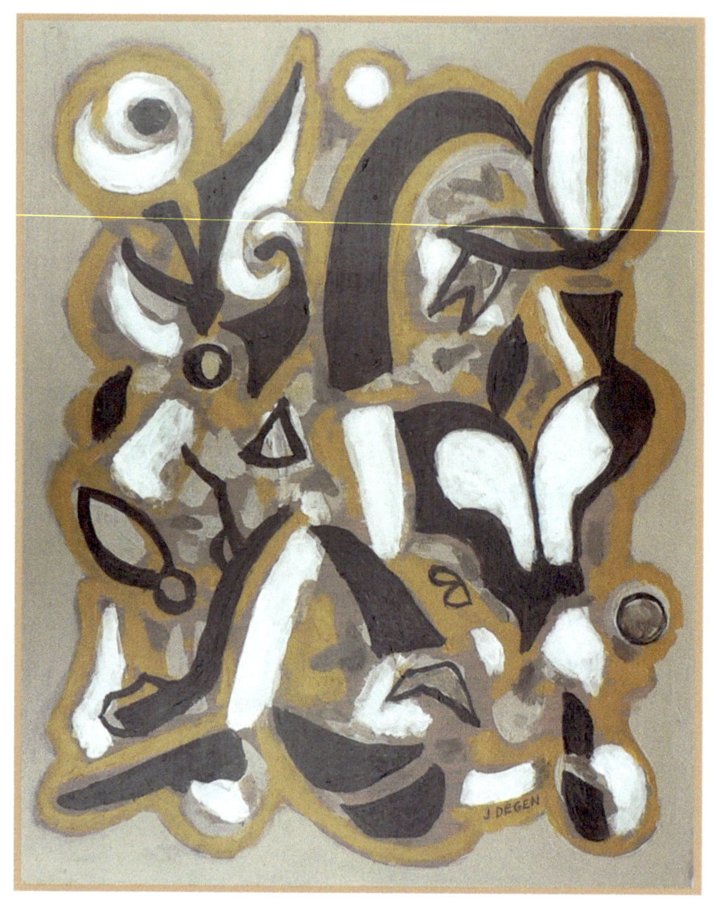

Twilight

Acrylic on board, 52 x 40 cm, 2012

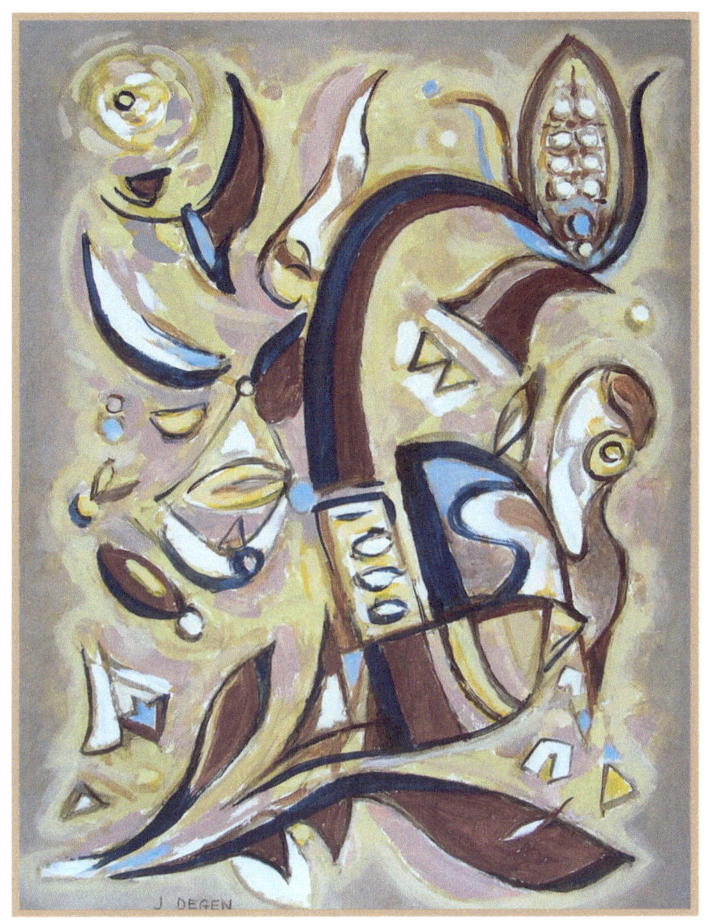

Impromtu

Oil on board, 56 x 40 cm, 2007

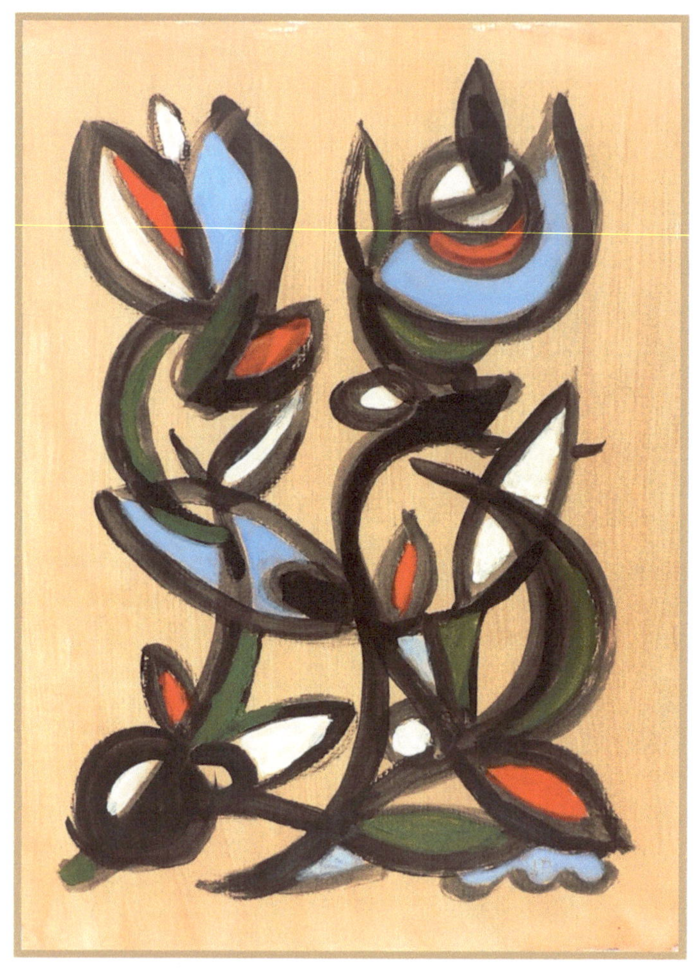

Growing Together

Acrylic on paper, 39 x 27 cm, 2009

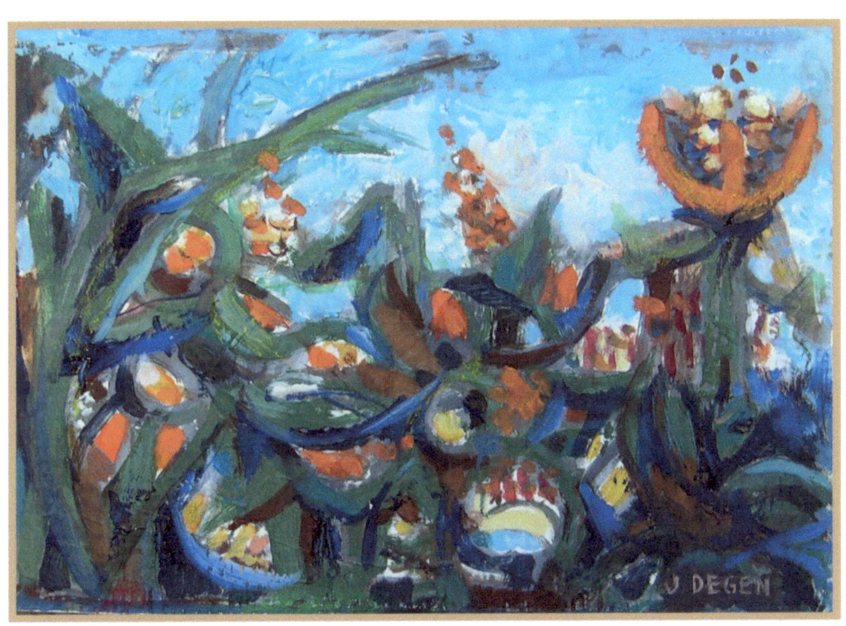

Green and Orange

Oil on board, 26 x 37 cm, 2008

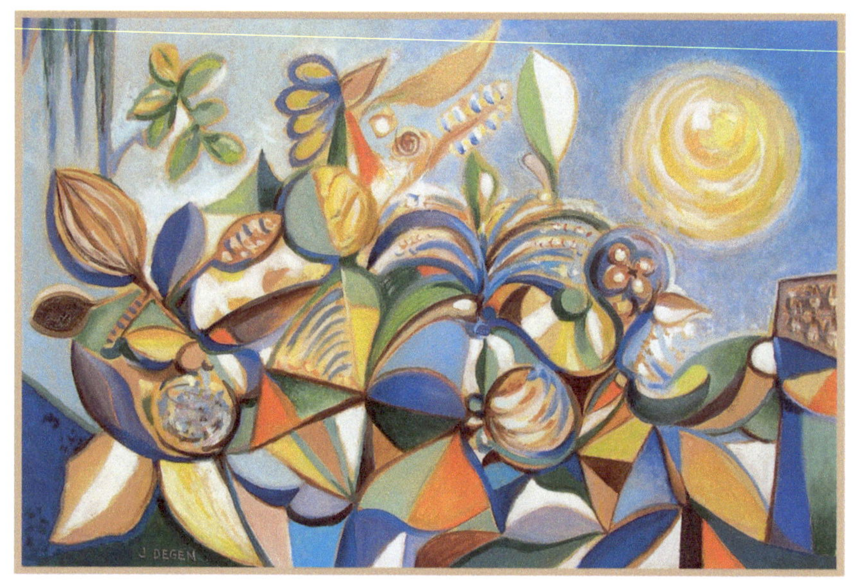

Floral Abstract

Acrylic on paper, 30 x 40 cm, 2011

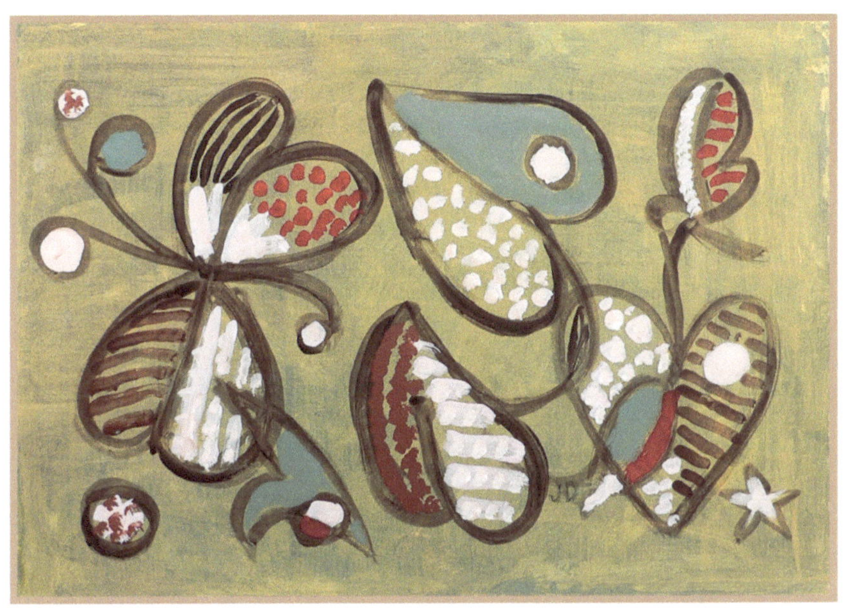

Gentle Flowering

Acrylic on paper, 26 x 36 cm, 2003

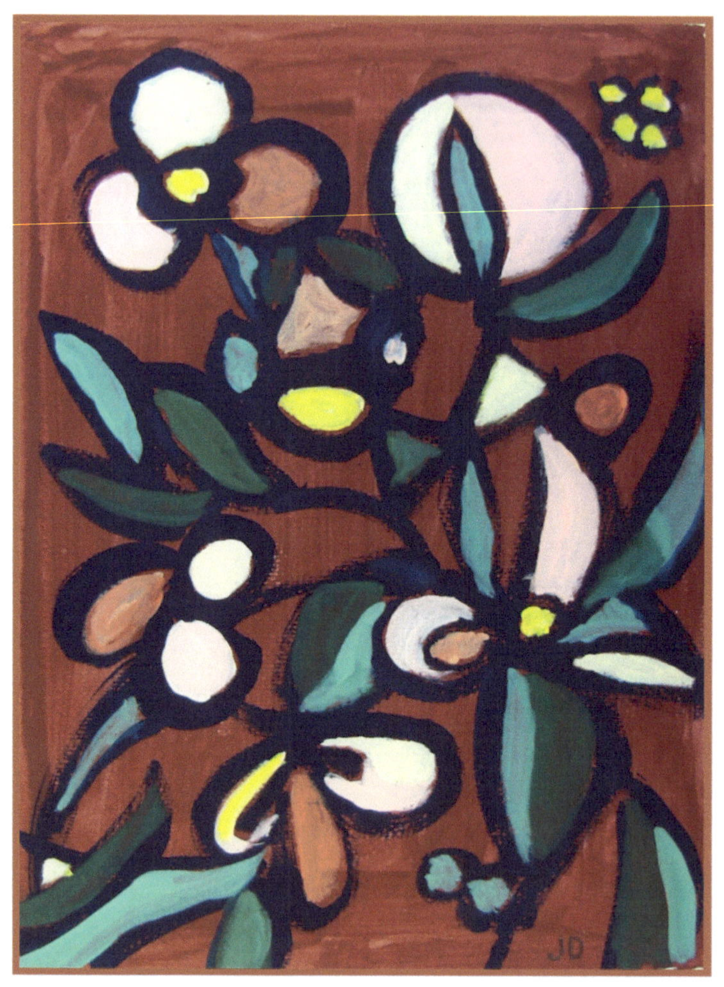

Earth Flowers

Acrylic on paper, 38 x 28 cm, 2008

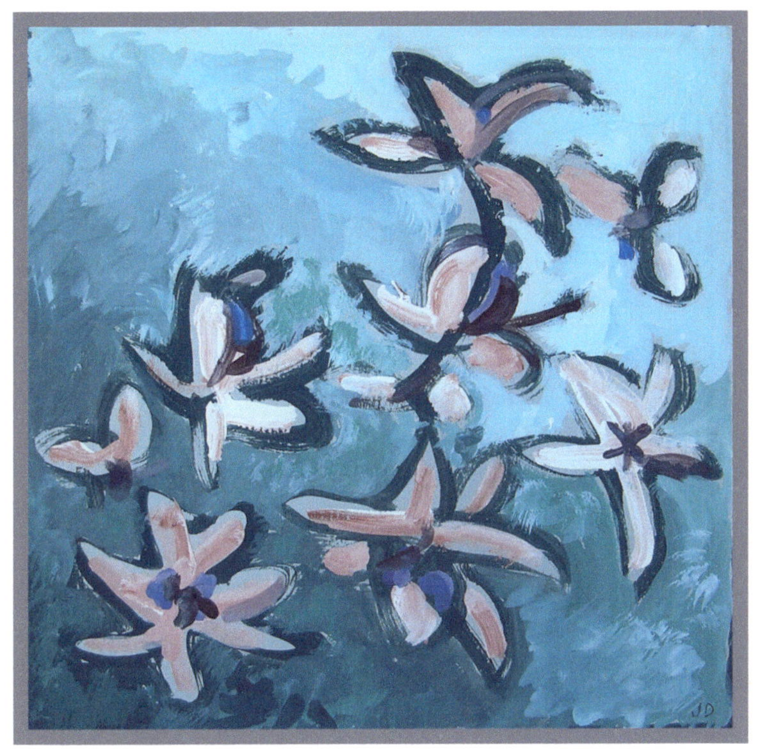

Pink Flowers

Acrylic on paper, 35 x 35 cm, 2007

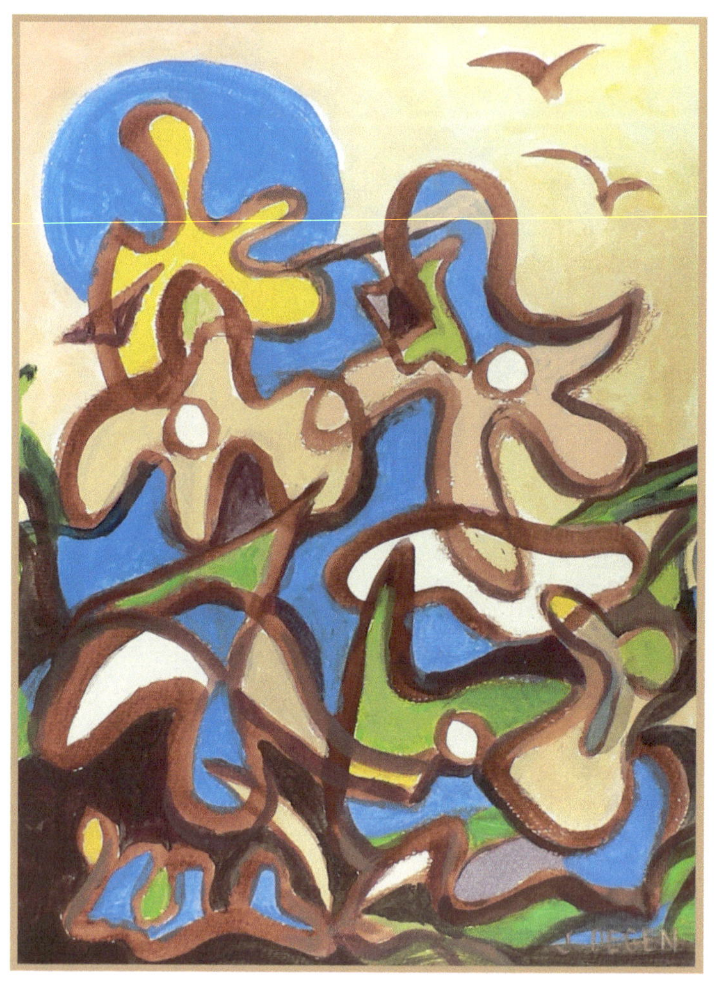

Blue Sun

Acrylic on paper, 39 x 28 cm, 2008

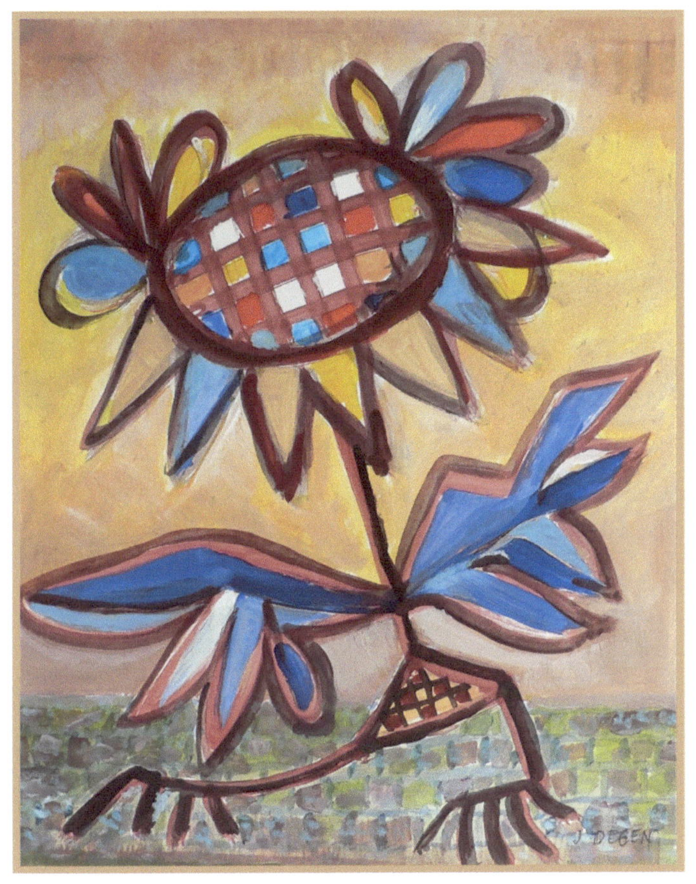

Flower on the Move

Acrylic on paper, 34 x 27 cm, 2010

*Art is an adventure into an unknown world,
which can only be explored by those
willing to take the risks.*
(Mark Rothko)

*No great artist ever sees things as they really are,
if he did he would cease to be an artist.*
(Oscar Wilde)

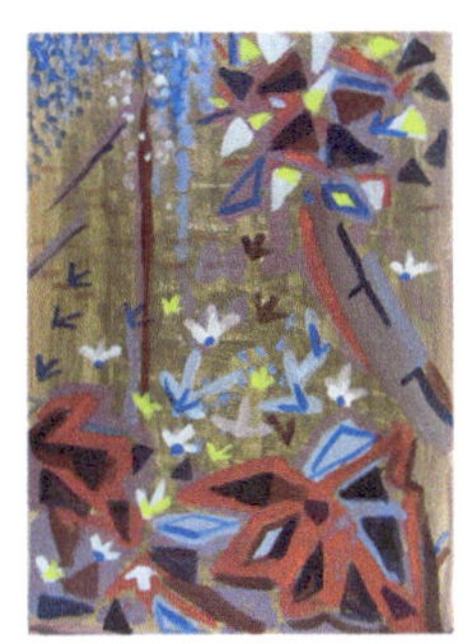

Fantasy

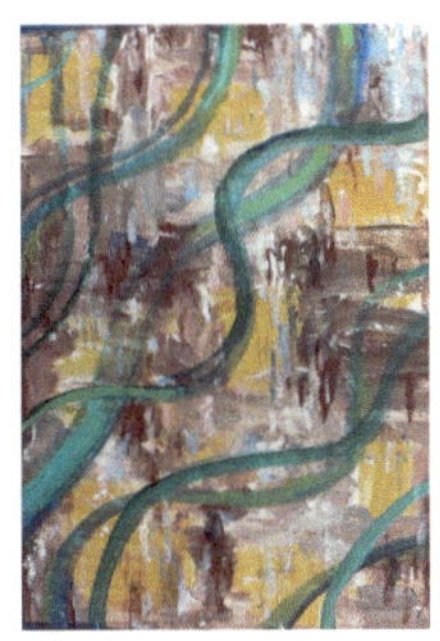

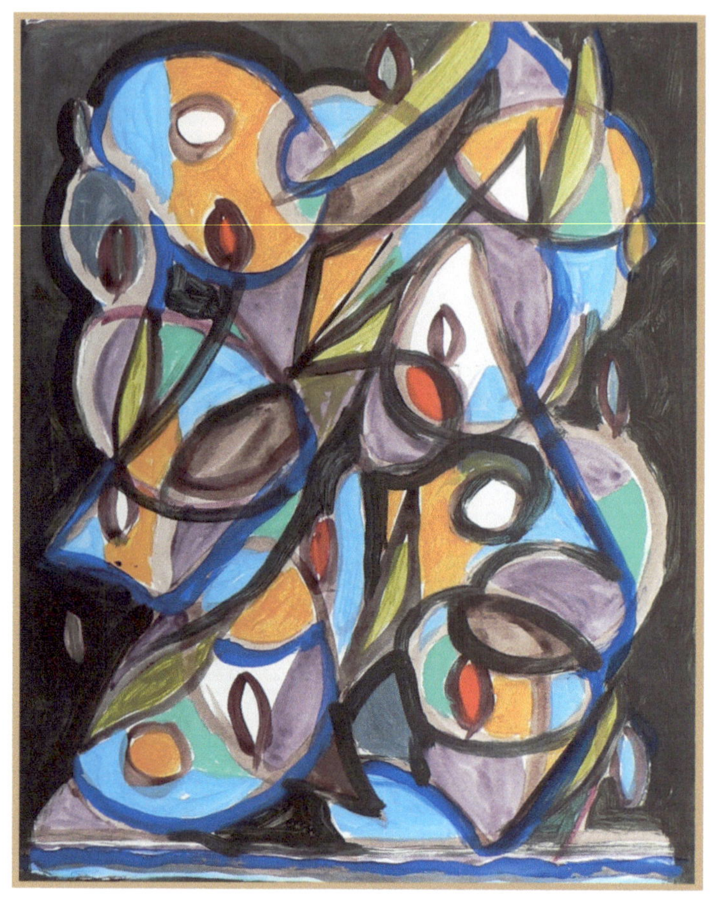

Forgotten Memories

Acrylic on paper, 37 x 29 cm, 2007

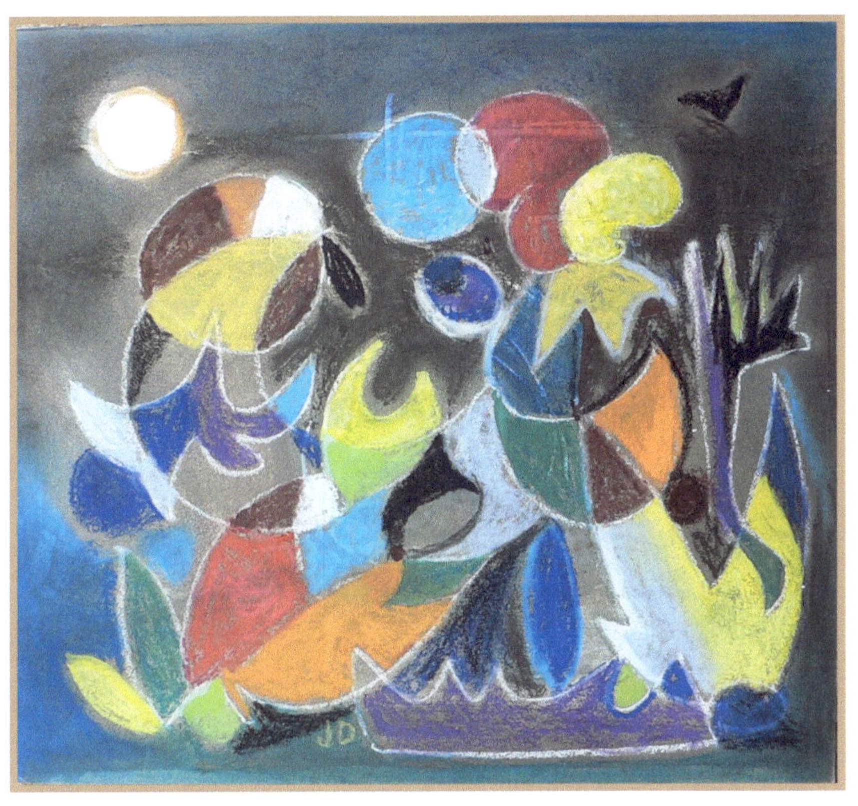

At Night

Pastel on paper, 28 x 28 cm, 2004

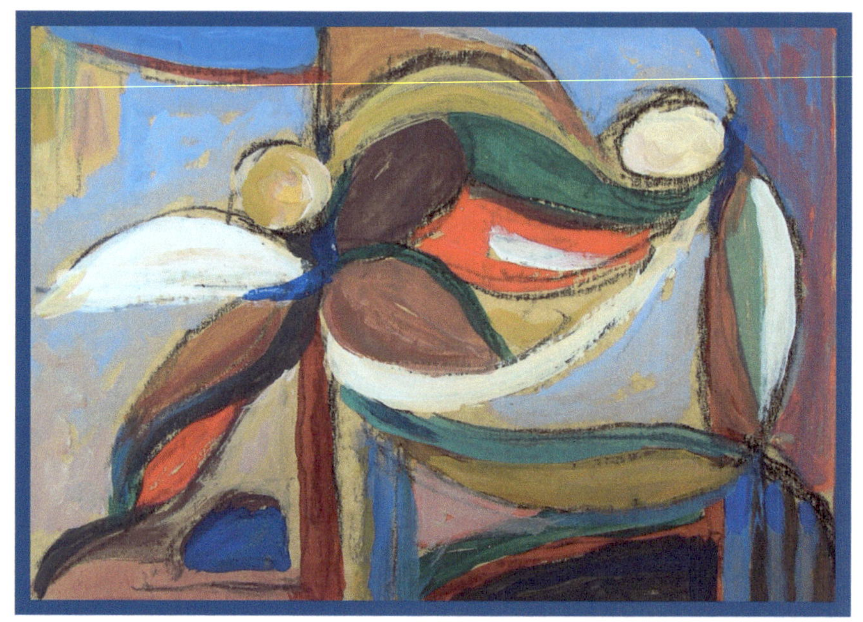

Flower Abstract

Oil on board, 18 x 24 cm, 2010

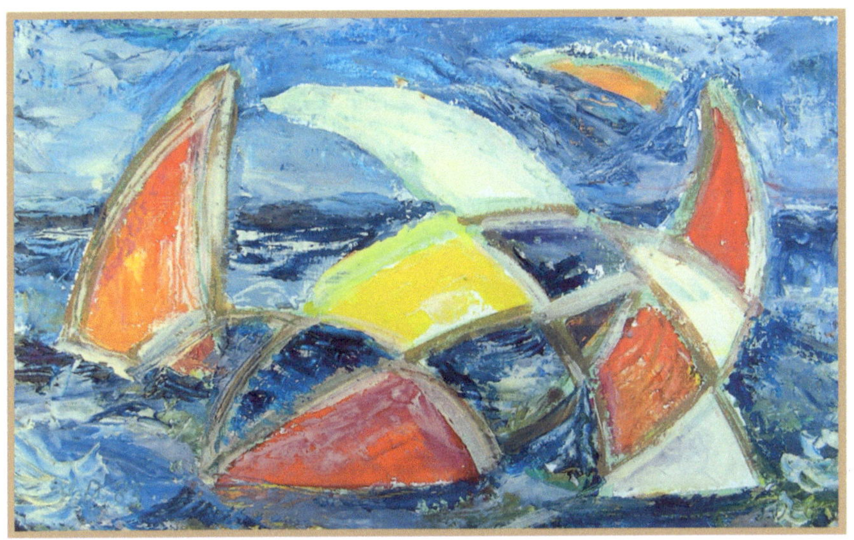

Boats in a Squall

Oil on board, 25 x 37 cm, 2002

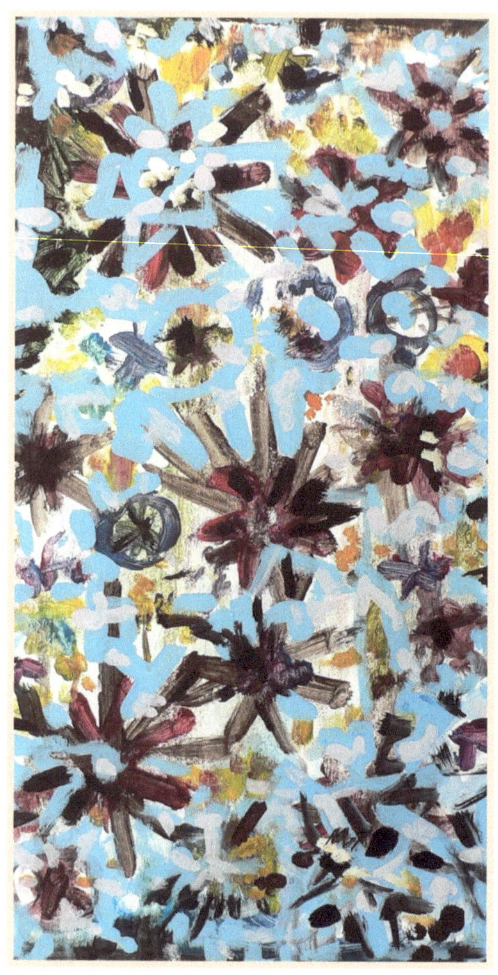

Flowers Aplenty

Acrylic on board, 43 x 25 cm, 2008

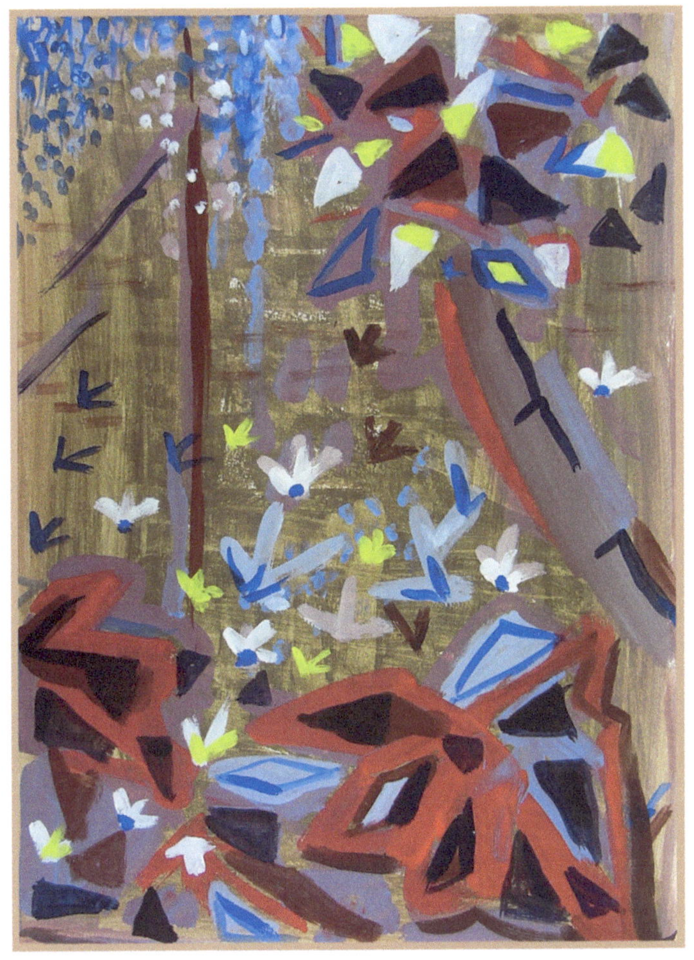

Garden Company

Acrylic on paper, 40 x 29 cm, 2005

146

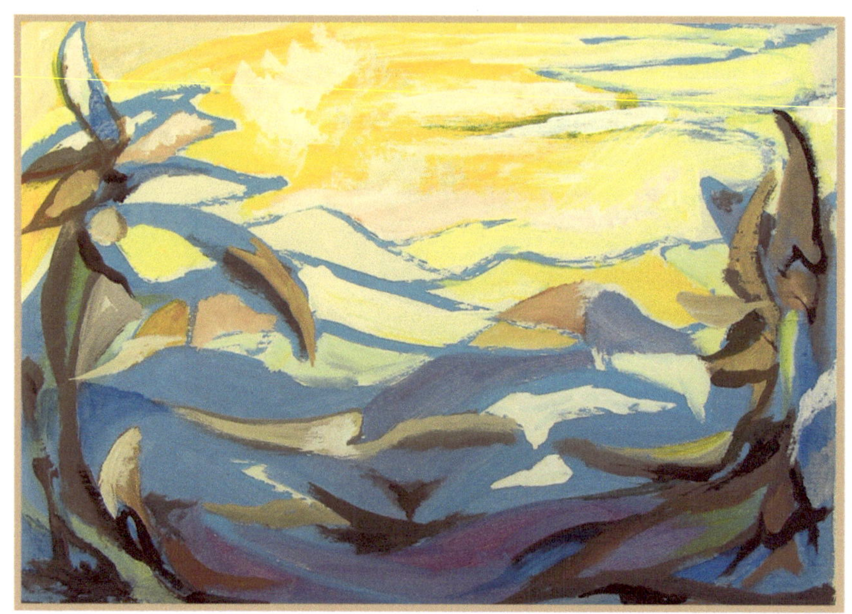

Yellow Sky

Acrylic on paper, 27 x 37 cm, 1982

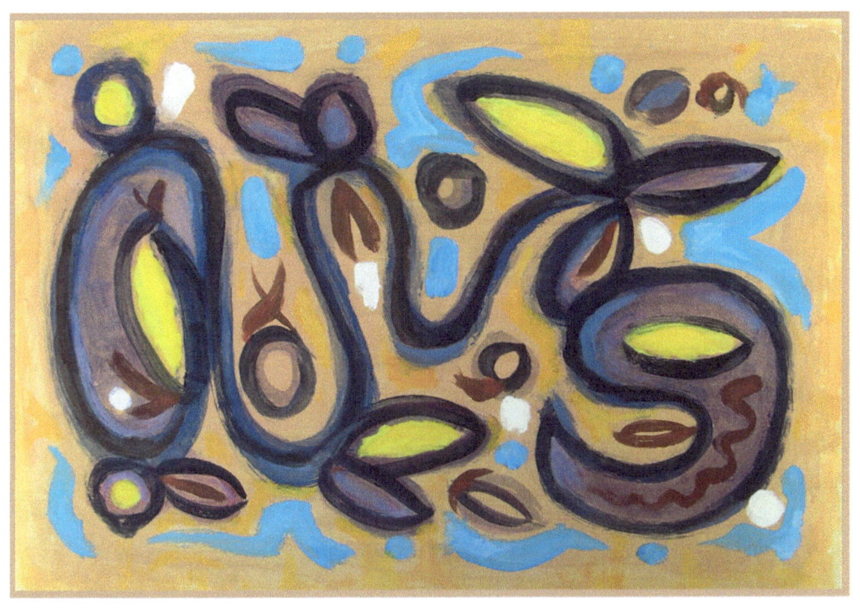

Flowers Resting

Acrylic on paper, 57 x 40 cm, 2007

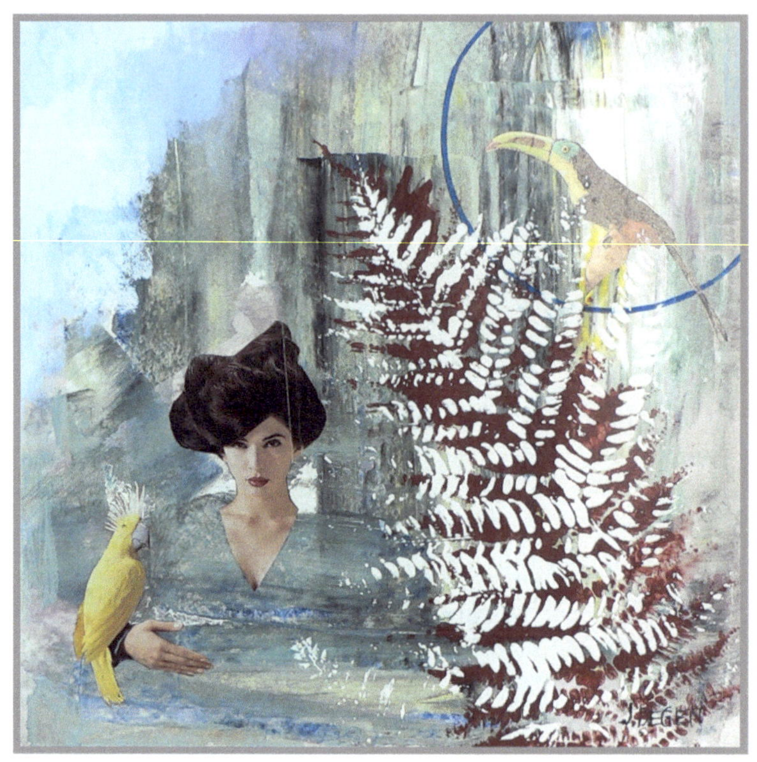

Lady and the Birds

Collage on paper, 25 x 24 cm, 2003

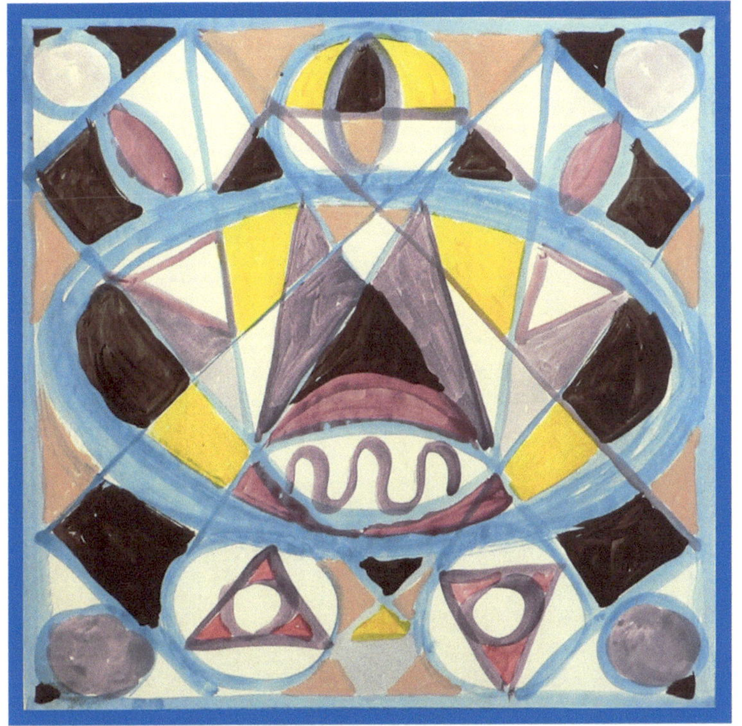

Blue Amethyst

Gouache on paper, 27 x 25 cm, 1992

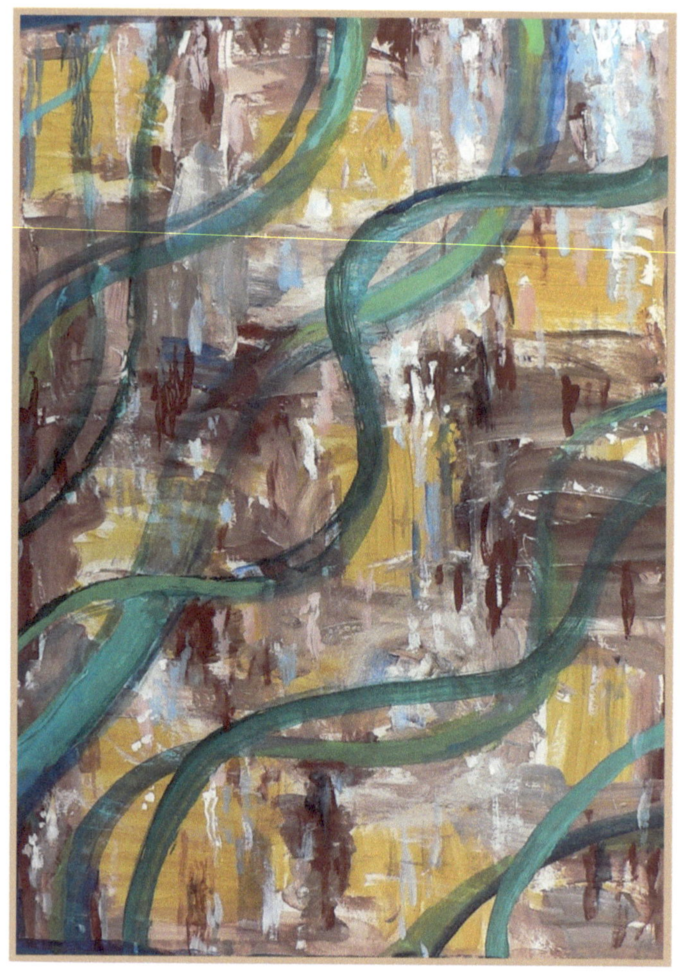

Fingers of Rain

Acrylic on paper, 39 x 27 cm, 2008

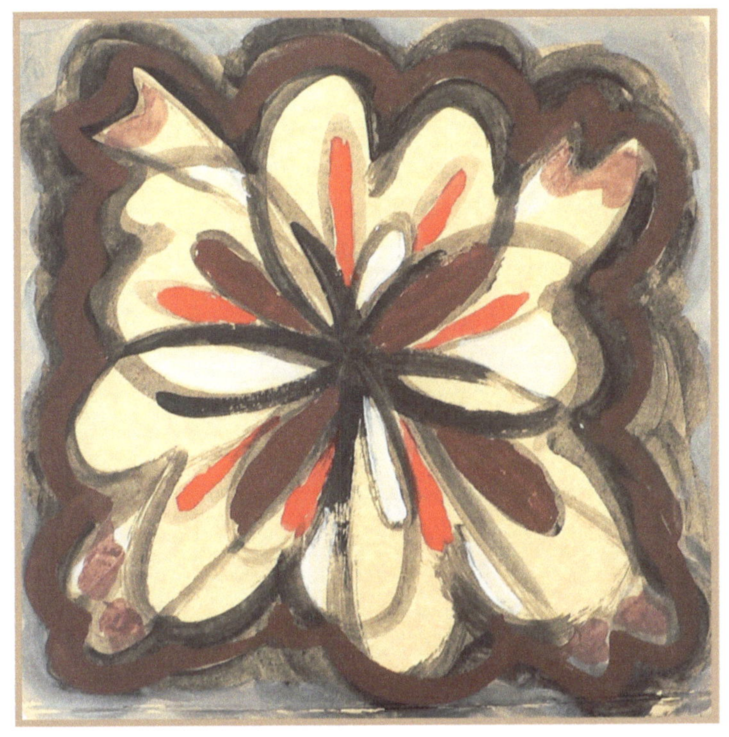

Autumn Flower

Acrylic on paper, 28 x 28 cm, 2005

MORE ABOUT JINDRICH'S OTHER BOOKS

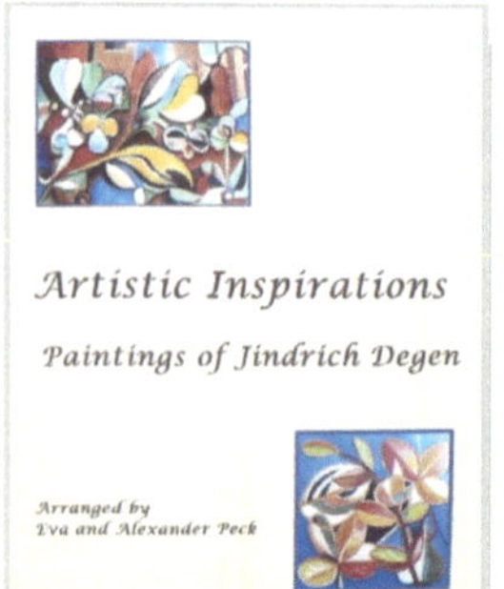

Artistic Inspirations – Paintings of Jindrich Degen The book features 200 of Jindrich (Henry) Degen's paintings. A range of diverse subjects is presented in both realistic and abstract art. The art works, produced in various media, are organized under twelve themes. This book is available in two editions – large (deluxe) and small (budget).

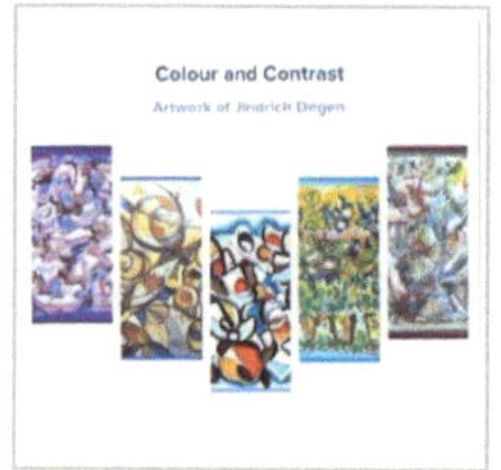

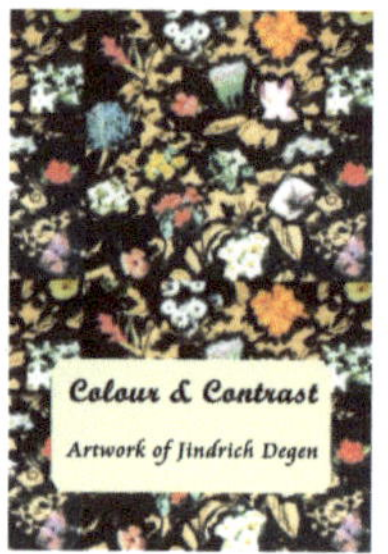

Colour and Contrast – Artwork of Jindrich Degen While the content is the same as for *Artistic Inspirations*, this book showcases each of Jindrich's art works on a separate page. Also available in a budget edition (→).

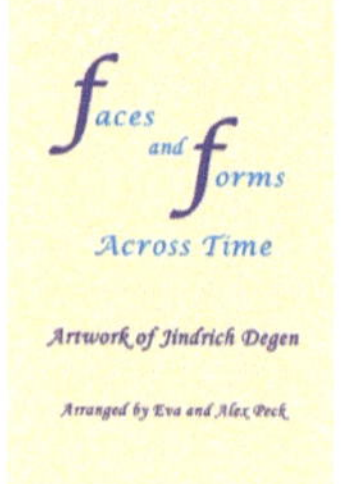

Faces and Forms Across Time is a selection of drawings and paintings of Jindrich (Henry) Degen featuring real-life portraits, and portraits drawn from photos or works of other artists; icons and symbols; wild and domestic animals; as well as products of Henry's imagination.

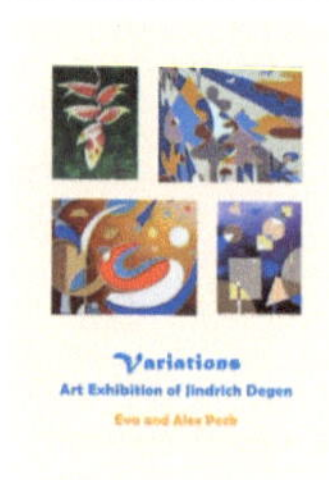

Variations documents an art exhibition of Jindrich (Henry) Degen held in November 2013 at the gallery of the Yurara Art Society in Thornlands, Queensland. It takes readers on a journey through an art show from preparation to packing up.

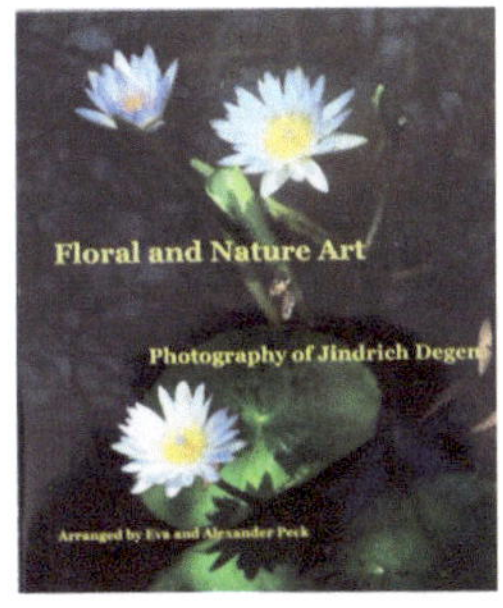

Floral and Nature Art – Photography of Jindrich Degen This book presents digital photography of Jindrich (Henry) Degen. The images of flowers and bushland settings, captured through the eyes of an artist, are arranged under the themes of floral art and nature art. Inspirational quotations on each page   complement the photographic beauty. Available in a large (deluxe) and a small (budget) editions.

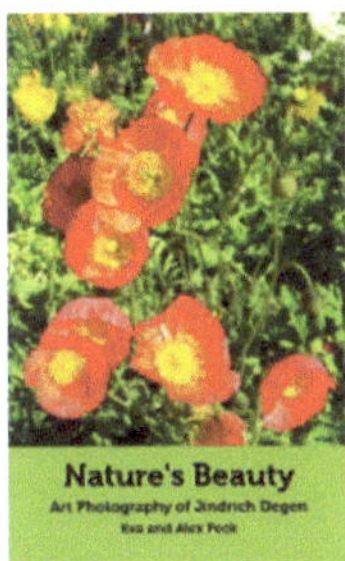

Nature's Beauty – Art Photography of Jindrich Degen This book features further digital photography of artist Jindrich (Henry) Degen. The images taken in natural settings of south-east Queensland reflect his imagination, giving many of his photos an artistic flair. The collection is arranged under ten themes and has complementing quotations on each page.

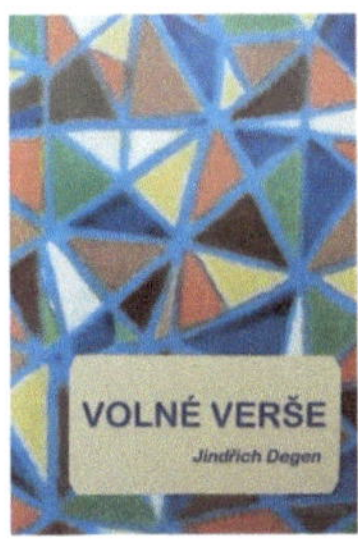

Volné verše (Free Verse) A diverse collection of Czech verse and prose, often in a light-hearted form, created over a decade and inspired by life's circumstances, this book addresses current issues of science and technology, as well as capturing experiences, dreams and fantasies of the author.

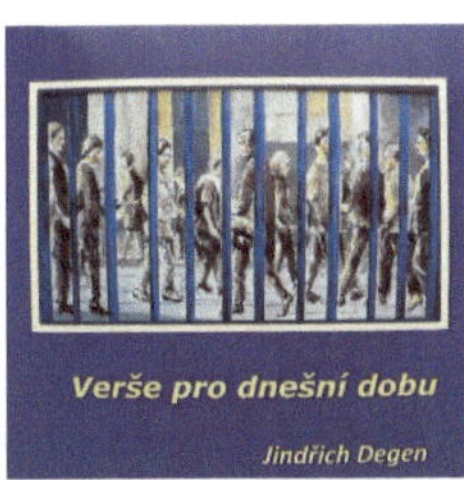

Verše pro dnešní dobu (Contemporary Verse) This small book is a selection of eleven works from *Volné verše*, presented as a graphically illustrated colour version. The verses speak to us today as much as in the time they were written.

ABOUT PATHWAY PUBLISHING

Pathway Publishing (www.pathway-publishing.org) is dedicated to sharing truth and beauty through books, as well as websites. It aims to present what is true to life and reality, as well as what is edifying and inspirational. The goal is to provide sound information and to lift the human spirit.

Pathway Publishing has a vision of helping readers on their path of enlightenment and spiritual transformation. The wisdom and experience of spiritual teachers, thinkers, and visionaries from various backgrounds and faith traditions are recognized and valued. Books produced by Pathway Publishing include:

- *Artistic Inspirations – Paintings of Jindrich Degen*, arranged by Eva and Alexander Peck (2011)

- *Colour and Contrast – Artwork of Jindrich Degen*, arranged by Eva and Alexander Peck (2013)

- *Faces and Forms Across Time – Artwork of Jindrich Degen*, arranged by Eva and Alex Peck (2013)

- *Variations – Art Exhibitions of Jindrich Degen*, arranged by Eva and Alex Peck (2013)

- *Floral and Nature Art – Photography of Jindrich Degen*, arranged by Eva and Alexander Peck (2011)

- *Nature's Beauty – Art Photography of Jindrich Degen*, arranged by Eva and Alex Peck (2013)

- *Memories of Times with Dad – Poems and Letters*, Alexander and Eva Peck (2011)

- *Volné verše*, Jindrich Degen (in Czech) (2012)

- *Verše pro dnešní dobu*, Jindrich Degen (in Czech) ((2011)

- *Divine Reflections in Times and Seasons*, Eva Peck (2013)

- *Divine Reflections in Natural Phenomena*, Eva Peck (2013)

- *Divine Reflections in Living Things*, Eva Peck (2013)

- *Divine Insights from Human Life*, Eva Peck (2013)

- *Pathway to Life – Through the Holy Scriptures*, Eva and Alexander Peck (2011)

- *Journey to the Divine Within – Through Silence, Stillness and Simplicity*, Alexander and Eva Peck (2011)

Some of the publications are also available as e-books.

For details of both books and websites, visit
www.pathway-publishing.org

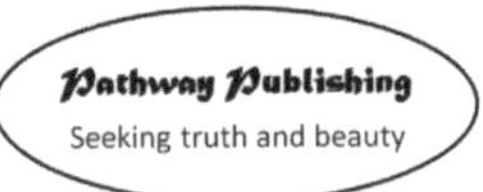